CROSSING THE SANDS

Wilfred Thesiger

WILFRED THESIGER

CROSSING THE SANDS

MOTIVATE
PUBLISHING

To my old friend Sheikh Zayed bin Sultan Al Nahyan, now the President of the United Arab Emirates, who offered me his hospitality in Abu Dhabi more than fifty years ago and has made me welcome there ever since.

Published by
Motivate Publishing

PO Box 2331, Dubai, UAE
PO Box 43072, Abu Dhabi, UAE
Macmillan House, 96 Kensington High Street, London W8 4SG

Directors: Obaid Humaid Al Tayer and Ian Fairservice
Editors: Ian Fairservice, Catherine Demangeot, Kate John
Art Director: Warren Jackson
Designer: Johnson Machado

First Published 1999 by Motivate Publishing

© Text and photographs Wilfred Thesiger

The original text from *Arabian Sands* is published by arrangement with HarperCollins Publishers Ltd.

ISBN 1 86063 028 6

British Library Cataloguing-in-Publication Data. A catalogue record for this book is available from the British Library.

Printed by Emirates Printing Press, Dubai, UAE.

Contents

Introduction

WILFRED THESIGER'S masterpiece, *Arabian Sands*, has remained continuously in print since it was first published by Longmans in 1959. 'Following worthily in the tradition of Burton, Doughty, Lawrence, Philby and Thomas', Lord Kinross concluded in the *Daily Telegraph*, 'it is, very likely, the book about Arabia to end all books about Arabia.' According to Hammond Innes, *Arabian Sands* was 'that rare thing, a really great travel book', while Sir John Glubb, praising its 'vividly written narrative', acknowledged Thesiger as 'perhaps the last, and certainly one of the greatest, of the British travellers among the Arabs.'

Arabian Sands celebrated Thesiger's travels with the Bedu, whose comradeship had given him 'the five happiest years of (his) life.' Twice, with small parties of Bait Kathir, Rashid and Saar tribesmen, he crossed the great southern desert: an area of almost half a million square miles, stretching from the Yemen border to Oman; from the southern coast of Arabia to the Arabian Gulf and the Nejd. Within it lay the vast wilderness of sand, 'a desert within a desert', Thesiger wrote, 'so enormous and so desolate that even the Arabs call it the Rub al Khali or the Empty Quarter.'

The *Sands* of the book's title is a Bedu synonym for the Empty Quarter, 'the last large area of the world which still remained unknown' and uncrossed when, in 1929, T.E. Lawrence wrote to Lord Trenchard, then Marshall of the R.A.F., 'nothing but an airship can do it, and I want it to be one of ours which gets the plum.'

Thesiger commented in 1951: 'Many famous Arabian travellers had dreamed of this achievement, but the realization of the dream was reserved for Bertram Thomas and St John Philby. As the names of Amundsen and Scott will always be associated with the attainment of the South Pole, so will the names of Thomas and Philby be remembered in connection with the crossing of the Empty Quarter.'

In 1930, Bertram Thomas crossed the Empty Quarter from the south, starting in Dhaufar and ending in Qatar. Thesiger wrote: 'Thomas's object was to cross the Empty Quarter, an undertaking which no European had yet achieved, and naturally he crossed it by the easiest way, where the sand dunes were small and the wells, known to his Rashid guides, were frequent.' But, he added: 'To minimise Thomas's achievement … would be as unjustifiable as to depreciate the first ascent of a great mountain because it was climbed by the easiest face.' By contrast, Thesiger tells us, the route from the north taken by St John Philby in 1931 'was far more difficult and the 400 miles between wells which he covered across the western sands at the end of his journeys will always be an epic of desert travel.'

Thesiger first crossed the Empty Quarter in 1946–47, aged 36, beginning and ending his journeys at Salala. On his second crossing, 1947–48, from Manwakh, he passed through Salaiyil — where he was detained by order of Ibn Saud, but released due to Philby's intervention— and ended at Abu Dhabi, then a small village on the Trucial Coast. The physical demands of the first crossing, faced by dunes more than 700 feet high, Thesiger still maintains, were the hardest he ever endured. During the second crossing, when his party travelled for 15 days without finding water, Thesiger's life had been threatened by fanatical tribes enraged by the presence of an infidel.

Overcoming the hardships, dangers and the mental challenge of these journeys gave him incomparable, deeply personal rewards. In the desert, he experienced 'a freedom unattainable in civilization'; 'tranquillity'; 'the satisfaction that comes from hardship'; 'the pleasure that springs from abstinence.' 'The Empty Quarter', Thesiger wrote, 'offered me the chance to win distinction as a traveller.' But more than this, 'in those empty wastes (he found) the peace that comes with solitude, and among the Bedu, comradeship in a hostile land.'

An established classic of modern travel, combining history, portraiture and autobiography, *Arabian Sands* has immortalized Thesiger's Bedu companions, Salim bin Kabina and Salim bin Ghabaisha, to whom it was dedicated. Thesiger's coda, a lament for the Bedu's vanished way of life, embodies what another writer defined as 'the clash of ancient and modern forces … which ignites the author's passion.'

In his opening chapter, Thesiger ponders the 'strange compulsion', the 'perverse necessity', which drove him 'from (his) own land to the deserts of the East.' Thesiger's intriguing dilemma leads to a résumé of his childhood in Ethiopia (then Abyssinia); his preparatory schooldays in Sussex, followed by Eton and Oxford; his return to Ethiopia for Haile Selassie's coronation, in 1930, and again, in 1933–34, when he successfully explored the Awash river; his influential years in the Sudan, 1935–39; finally, his wartime activities in Ethiopia, the Middle East and North Africa. Thesiger ended the chapter: 'All my past had been but a prelude to the five years that lay ahead of me.'

These desert years would become the *raison d'être* of *Arabian Sands*. Yet, Thesiger confessed: 'During the years that I was in Arabia, I never thought that I would write a book about my travels. Had I done so, I should have kept fuller notes which now would have helped and hindered me. Seven years after leaving Arabia, I showed some photographs I had taken to (the literary agent) Graham Watson, and he strongly urged me to write a book about the desert. This I refused to do. I realized that

it would involve me in much hard work, and I did not wish to settle down in Europe for a couple of years when I could be travelling in countries that interested me. The following day, Graham Watson came to see me again, and this time he brought Mark Longman with him. After much argument, the two of them persuaded me to try to write this book. Now that I have finished it I am grateful to them, for the effort to remember every detail has brought back vividly into my mind the Bedu amongst whom I travelled, and the vast empty land across which I rode on camels for ten thousand miles.'

Thesiger wrote *Arabian Sands* during 1957–58 in Denmark and Ireland. As the book progressed, he sent chapters to Graham Watson and his friend Val ffrench Blake, who read them critically and offered advice. Thesiger gradually developed a sparse, elegant prose style which perfectly matched his theme, and has since become his hallmark.

It is interesting to reflect that Watson had first visited Wilfred Thesiger in 1956 with the then remote possibility of a book of photographs in mind. Now, after more than 40 years, this illustrated edition, *Crossing the Sands*, pays a fitting tribute to the original and, at the same time, brings the publishing history of *Arabian Sands* full circle.

The Author with his companions during the first crossing of the Empty Quarter.

Prelude in Dhaufar

The Wali of Dhaufar collects a party of Bait Kathir at Salala to escort me to the Sands of Ghanim. While waiting for their arrival I travel in the Qarra mountains.

The deserts of Arabia cover more than a million square miles, and the southern desert occupies nearly half of the total area. The southern desert stretches for nine hundred miles from the frontier of the Yemen to the foothills of Oman, and for five hundred miles from the southern coast of Arabia to the Gulf and the borders of the Najd.

It would have been difficult, perhaps even impossible, for me to have approached the Empty Quarter without the initial backing which I received from the Middle East Anti-Locust Unit, but once I had been there and had made friends with the Bedu I could travel where I wished, I had no need to worry about international boundaries that did not even exist on maps.

I arrived in Aden at the end of September 1945, visited the mountains along the Yemen frontier, and on 15 October flew to Salala, the capital of Dhaufar, which lies about two-thirds of the way along the southern coast of Arabia. It was from there that I was to start my journey. While at Salala I stayed with the R.A.F. in their camp outside the town. It was on a bare stony plain which was shut in by the Qarra mountains a few miles away, and had been set up during the war when an air route from Aden to India was opened. This route was no longer used, but once a week an aeroplane came to Salala from Aden.

As I entered the town of Salala I passed a small caravan, two men with four camels tied head to tail, and when I questioned the guard who was with me he said that these camels were carrying *mughur*, or frankincense. My attention was caught by the men who led the camels. They were small and wiry, about five feet four inches in height, and were dressed in a length of dark-blue cloth wound round their waists, with an end thrown over one shoulder. They were bare-headed, and their hair was long and untidy. Both of them wore daggers and carried rifles. My guard said that they were Bedu from beyond the mountains and that they belonged to the Bait Kathir. In the market-place were more of them, while others waited outside the palace gates.

The gates were guarded by armed men dressed in long Arab shirts and head-cloths. Some of them were from Oman and the

The greater part of the southern desert is a wilderness of sand; it is a desert within a desert, so enormous and so desolate that even Arabs call it the Rub al Khali or the Empty Quarter.

Dhow at Aden.

rest were slaves; none were local tribesmen. One of them took me into the reception hall, where I met the Wali. He was a townsman from Oman, large and portly. He was dressed in a white shirt reaching to the ground, a brown cloak, embroidered with gold, and a Kashmiri shawl which was loosely wrapped round his head. He wore a large curved dagger at the middle of his stomach. I greeted him in Arabic, and before we started our discussion I ate a few dates and drank three cups of bitter black coffee handed to me by one of his retainers.

The Wali told me that he had been instructed by the Sultan to collect a party of Bedu with camels to take me to Mughshin. He said that he had arranged for forty-five Bedu to go with me and that now he would send messengers into the desert to fetch them. I thanked him, but suggested that a dozen would be quite enough. I knew that the British Consul in Muscat, when he got permission for me to do this journey, had agreed with the Sultan that the size of the party should be fixed by the Wali, and that I was to pay the equivalent of ten shillings a day to each man who went with me. I realized that everyone here regarded my journey as a heaven-sent opportunity to enrich himself, and that they would all try to make my party as large as possible. The Wali now insisted that, as there was a serious risk of my meeting raiders, he could not take the responsibility of allowing me to go to Mughshin with fewer than forty-five men, and that the Bedu themselves would not agree to go with a smaller party.

Eventually, after several meetings with the Wali I agreed to take thirty Arabs. The Wali told me they would be from the Bait Kathir tribe, and added that they would be ready to start in a fortnight.

I arranged to spend this time travelling in the Qarra mountains, which had been explored by Theodore and Mabel Bent in 1895 and by Bertram Thomas in 1929. The Wali said that he would send four of his retainers with me, two Omanis and two slaves, and that we should have to hire camels from the Qarra, who live in the mountains, changing them every time we crossed from one valley into the next, since each valley was owned by a different section of the tribe.

Two days later we rode our camels across the stony plain of Jarbib; we passed some cultivation and went on towards Jabal Qarra, which is about two thousand feet high, and is flanked on either side by much higher mountains which close in on the sea.

We camped in the mouth of a valley near a Qarra village. I stayed there for ten days. Then I heard rumours that the Bait Kathir, who were to go with me, were in Salala, and I decided to go back.

On my return the Wali invited me to meet some of the Bait Kathir who were to go with me. There were eight of them sitting with him when I arrived. Six wore head-cloths and Arab shirts reaching half-way down their calves; two were bareheaded and dressed only in loin-cloths. All wore daggers and cartridge belts; they had left their rifles outside the audience hall. While we drank coffee and ate dates I wondered how I should get on with these people. An old man with a fringe of white beard and twinkling eyes, Salim Tamtaim, was their head sheikh. The Wali said he was eighty, but still vigorous, having just married another wife; and the old man exclaimed 'Eh, by God, I can still ride and shoot.' I noticed especially a man called Sultan to whom the others deferred rather than to Tamtaim, and I remembered that the Qarra had said: 'Sultan has arrived in Salala with the Bait Kathir.' It was obvious that he was their leader. The Wali pointed to another of them and said: 'Musallim will shoot meat for you. He is famous as a hunter.' The man of whom he spoke was dressed in a clean white shirt, and an embroidered head-cloth. He was a small man, like all the others, but he was more solidly built and slightly bow-legged. He looked more of a townsman than a Bedu. I arranged with them that they should fetch me next morning from the R.A.F. camp.

To my unpractised eye the Qarra were similar in appearance to the Bait Kathir whom I had seen in Salala, but they spoke their own language, whereas the Bait Kathir spoke Arabic. Three tribes, the Qarra, Mahra, and Harasis, as well as the remnants of others like the Shahara, speak different dialects of a common origin and are known to the Arabic-speaking tribes as the Ahl al Hadara.

Sultan looked more like an American Red Indian than an Arab. He had a striking face, austere, lined, and hairless, except for a few hairs growing in a curl on his chin.

They arrived after breakfast accompanied by a large crowd from Salala. They were a wild-looking lot, most of them wearing only loin-cloths, and all of them armed with rifles and daggers. I showed old Tamtaim and Sultan the food I had provided for the journey — rice, flour, dates, sugar, tea, coffee, and liquid butter. With the help of the R.A.F. storeman I had done it up in sacks in what seemed to me suitable-sized loads, but Sultan said at once that they were too heavy. They undid them and started to repack, pouring the rice, flour, and sugar into dirty-looking goatskin bags. They argued endlessly among themselves, shouting in harsh voices. The camels were led up and couched, but they struggled roaring to their feet, and were couched again.

When they were nearly ready I went into the hut where I had been staying and put on my Arab clothes. To have worn European clothes would have alienated these Bait Kathir at once, for although a few of them had travelled with Bertram Thomas, most of them had not even spoken to an Englishman before. I wore a loin-cloth, a long shirt, and a head-cloth with the ends twisted round my head in their fashion. None of these Bait Kathir wore the black woollen head-rope which is a conspicuous feature of Arab dress in the north.

On previous journeys I had commanded respect as an Englishman, and in the Sudan I had the prestige of being a government official. When I had travelled in the desert there I had tried to break through the barrier that lay between me and my companions, but I had always felt rather condescending. Now for the first time I was travelling without a servant. Quite alone among a crowd of Arabs whom I had never seen before, I should be with them for three or four months, even for six if I undertook the second journey to the Hadhramaut which I was already planning. At first glance they seemed to be little better than savages, as primitive as the Danakil, but I was soon disconcerted to discover that, while they were prepared to tolerate me as a source of very welcome revenue, they never doubted my inferiority. They were Muslims and Bedu and I was neither. They had never heard of the English, for all Europeans were known to them simply as Christians, or more probably infidels, and nationality had no meaning for them. They had heard vaguely of the war as a war between the Christians, and of the Aden government as a Christian government. Their world was the desert and they had little if any interest in events that happened outside it. They identified me with the Christians from Aden, but had no idea of any power greater than that of Ibn Saud. One day they spoke of a sheikh in the Hadhramaut who had recently defied the government and against whom the Aden levies had carried out some rather inconclusive operations. I realized that they thought that this force was all that my tribe could muster. They judged power by the number and effectiveness of fighting men, not by machines which they could not understand.

As this was the first time I had worn Arab dress I felt extremely self-conscious. My shirt was new, white, and rather stiff, very noticeable among the Bedu's dingy clothes. They were all small men, and as I am six foot two I felt as conspicuous as a lighthouse, and as different from them as one of the R.A.F.

I shall always remember the first camp at the foot of the Qarra mountains. We had stopped in a shallow watercourse which ran out into the plain, and we had dumped our kit wherever there was room for it among thorn bushes and boulders. The others were soon busy, greasing water-skins, twisting rope, mending saddles, and looking to their camels. I sat near them, conscious of their scrutiny. I longed to go over to and join them in their tasks, but I was kept awkwardly apart by my reserve. For the first and last time I felt lonely in Arabia.

I asked them about the Rub al Khali, or the Empty Quarter, the goal of my ambitions. No-one had heard of it. 'What is he talking about? What does he want?' 'God alone knows. I cannot understand his talk.' At last Sultan exclaimed 'Oh! he means the Sands', and I realized that this was their name for the great desert of southern Arabia. I have heard townsmen and villagers in the Najd and the Hajaz refer to it as the Rub al Khali, but never Bedu who lived upon its borders.

I found it difficult to understand their talk. In the Sudan I had learnt Arabic among tribes who spoke it as their second language. I had really only begun to speak it when I was in Syria during the war. But there was a great difference between Syrian Arabic and the dialect of the Bait Kathir, whose pronunciation and intonation were entirely different from anything I had heard before, and many of whose words were archaic. The Bait Kathir were equally puzzled by my speech, but this did not stop them from asking questions about 'The Christians'. 'Did they know God? Did they fast and pray? Were they circumcised? Did they marry like Muslims or just take a woman when they wanted one? How much bride-price did they pay? Did they own camels? Were they tribesmen? How did they bury their dead?' It was always questions such as these that they asked me. None of them had any interest in the cars and aeroplanes which they had seen in the R.A.F. camp. The rifles with which they fought were all that they had accepted from the outside world, the only modern invention which interested them.

They spoke of Bertram Thomas who had travelled with them. Bedu notice everything and forget nothing. Garrulous by nature, they reminisce endlessly, whiling away with their chatter the long marching hours, and talking late into the night round their camp fires. Their life is at all times desperately hard, and they are merciless critics of those who fall short in patience, good humour, generosity, loyalty, or courage. They make no allowance for the stranger. Whoever lives with the Bedu must accept Bedu conventions, and conform to Bedu standards. Only those who have journeyed with them can appreciate the strain of such a life. These tribesmen are accustomed since birth to the physical hardships of the desert, to drink the scanty bitter water of the Sands, to eat gritty unleavened bread, to endure the maddening irritation of driven sand, intense cold, heat, and blinding glare in a land without shade or cloud. But more wearing still is the nervous tension. I was to learn how hard it is to live crowded together with people of another faith, speech, and culture in the solitude of the desert, how easy to be provoked to senseless wrath by the importunities and improvidence.

The Sands of Ghanim

After travelling to the Sands of Ghanim and Mughshin we return to Salala. There I meet the Rashid for the first time and travel with them to the Hadhramaut.

This first journey on the fringes of the Empty Quarter was only important to me as my probation for the far longer and more difficult journeys that were to follow. During the next five months I learnt to adapt myself to Bedu ways and to the rhythm of their life.

We drifted along, our movements governed by an indefinable common consent. There was seldom much discussion; we either halted or we went on. Sometimes we would start in the morning, come unexpectedly on grazing soon after we had started, and halt for the day. At other times we planned to stop somewhere, but finding there was no grazing, we would push on without a halt till dark or even later. If we stopped in the middle of the day we would hurriedly unload the camels, hobble them, and turn them loose to graze. Then we might cook bread or porridge, but more often we ate dates. Always we drank coffee. Some of them smoked, and this was their only other indulgence. No-one ever smoked without sharing his pipe with the others; they would squat round while one sifted a few grains of tobacco from the dust in the bottom of a small leather bag which he carried inside his shirt next to his skin. He would stuff this tobacco into a small stemless pipe cut out of soft stone, or into an old cartridge case open at both ends, light it with a flint and steel, take two or three deep puffs and hand it to the next person. If we were travelling when they wished to smoke, they stopped, got off, squatted down, smoked and then climbed back into their saddles.

In Darfur I had fed my camels on grain and had trotted them. In southern Arabia the Bedu never trot when they are on a journey, for their camels eat only what they can find, which is generally very little, and have to travel long distances between wells. I had already learnt on the journeys to Bir Natrun and to Tibesti not to press a camel beyond its normal walking pace when travelling in the desert.

I was soon to discover how considerate the Bedu were of their camels, always ready to suffer hardship themselves in order to spare their animals. Several times while travelling with them and approaching a well, I have expected them to push on and fill the water-skins, as our water was finished, but they have insisted on halting for the night short of the well, saying that farther on there was no grazing. We always walked for the first two or three hours. While we were still in the mountains each of us led his camel, or tied her by her head-rope to the tail of the one in front. Later, when we were on the gravel plains or in the sands, we turned them loose to find whatever food they could as they drifted along. When at length the sun grew hot we rode.

Whenever we passed any bushes we let our camels dawdle to strip mouthfuls of leaves and thorns, and whenever we came to richer grazing we halted to let them graze at will. I was making a time-and-compass traverse of our route and these constant halts were frustrating, making it difficult to estimate the distance which we had covered. On good going, where there was no feeding to delay us, we averaged three miles an hour, but in the Sands, where the dunes were steep and difficult, we might only do one mile an hour.

It often seemed incredible to me, especially when I was on foot and conscious of the steps I was taking, that we could cover such enormous distances going at this pace. Sometimes I counted my footsteps to a bush or to some other mark, and this number seemed but a trifle deducted from the sum that lay ahead of us. Yet I had no desire to travel faster. In this way there was time to notice things — a grasshopper under a bush, the tracks of a hare, a bird's nest, the shape and colour of ripples on the sand, the bloom of tiny seedlings pushing through the soil. I thought how terribly boring it would be to rush about this country in a car.

The Bedu either sit with a leg on either side of the hump, or kneel in the saddle, sitting on the upturned soles of their feet, in which case they are riding entirely by balance. They prefer to ride kneeling, especially if they mean to gallop. It is an extraordinary feat of balance, for riding a galloping camel, especially over rough ground, is like sitting on a bucking horse. A Bedu usually carries his rifle slung under his arm and parallel with the ground, which must add greatly to the difficulty of balancing. I could not ride kneeling; it was too uncomfortable and too precarious even at a walk.

With some of my companions, second left to right: Salim bin Amir, Musallim bin al Kamam, myself, Abdullah bin Misad and Sultan.

We always camped crowded together. All around us was endless space, and yet in our camps there was scarcely room to move, especially when the camels had been brought in for the night and couched around the fires. When we started on this journey we had divided ourselves into messes of five or six people, who each carried their own food. I fed with old Tamtaim, Sultan, and three others. One was Mabkhaut, a slightly built man of middle age; he was good-humoured and considerate, but he seldom spoke, which was unusual among these garrulous Bedu. Another was Musallim bin Tafl, who had been pointed out to me by the Wali as a skilful hunter. He was avaricious even by Bedu standards, quick-witted and hard-working. He was often in Salala, hanging about the palace, and had had in consequence the unusual experience of some contact with the outside world. He volunteered to do the cooking for our party.

When we had enough water he would cook rice, but generally he made bread for our evening meal. He would scoop out three or four pounds of flour from one of the goatskin bags in which we carried our supplies, and would then damp this, add a little salt and mix it into a thick paste. He would divide the dough into six equal-sized lumps, pat each lump between his hands until it had become a disc about half an inch thick, and would then put it down on a rug while he shaped the others. Someone else would have lighted the fire, sometimes with matches but generally with flint and steel. There was plenty of flint in the desert and the blade of a dagger to use as steel. They would tear small strips off their shirts or head-cloths for tinder, with the result that each day their clothes became more tattered in appearance. Musallim would rake some embers out of the fire to make a glowing bed, and then drop the cakes of dough on to it. The heat having sealed the outside of the cakes, he would turn them over almost immediately, and then, scooping a hollow in the sand under the embers, would bury them and spread the hot sand and embers over them. I would watch bubbles breaking through this layer of sand and ashes as the bread cooked. Later he would uncover the cakes, brush off the sand and ashes and put them aside to cool. When we wished to feed he would give one to each of us, and we would sit in a circle and, in turn, dip pieces of this bread into a small bowl containing melted butter, or soup if we happened to have anything from which to make it. The bread was brick hard or soggy, according to how long it had been cooked, and always tasted as if it had been made from saw dust. Sometimes Musallim shot a gazelle or an oryx, and only then did we feed well. After we had eaten we would sit round the fire and talk. Bedu always shout at each other, even if they are only a few feet apart. Everyone could therefore hear what was being said by everyone else in the camp, and anyone who was interested in a conversation round another fire could join in from where he was sitting.

Soon after dinner I would spread out my rug and sheepskin and putting my dagger and cartridge belt under the saddlebags which I used as a pillow, lie down beneath three blankets with my rifle beside me. While I was among the Arabs I was anxious to behave as they did, so that they would accept me to some extent as one of themselves. I had therefore to sit as they did, and I found this very trying, for my muscles were not accustomed to this position. I was glad when it was night and I could lie down and be at ease. I had sat on the ground before, but then I had been travelling with men whom I knew well, and with them I could relax and lie about. Now I would get off my camel after a long march and have to sit formally as Arabs sit. It took me a long time to get used to this. For the same reason I went barefooted as they did, and at first this was torture. Eventually the soles of my feet became hardened, but even after five years they were soft compared with theirs.

Muslims are usually very prudish and careful to avoid exposing themselves. My companions always kept their loin-cloths on even when they washed at the wells. At first I found it difficult to wear a loin-cloth with decency when sitting on the ground. Bedu say to anyone whose parts are showing, 'Your nose!' I had this said to me once or twice before I learnt to be more careful. The first time I wiped my nose thinking that there was a drip on the end of it, for the weather was very cold.

At first I found living with the Bedu very trying, and during the years that I was with them I always found the mental strain greater than the physical. It was as difficult for me to adapt myself to their way of life, and especially to their outlook, as it was for them to accept what they regarded as my eccentricities. I had been used to privacy, and here I had none. If I wanted to talk privately to someone it was difficult. Even if we went a little apart, others would be intrigued and immediately come to find out what we were talking about and join in the conversation. Every word I said was overheard, and every move I made was watched. At first I felt very isolated among them. I knew they thought that I had unlimited money, and I suspected that they were trying to exploit me. I was exasperated by their avarice, and wearied by their importunities. Whenever during these early days one of them approached me, I thought, 'Now what is *he* going to ask for?' and I would be irritated by the childish flattery with which they invariably prefaced their requests. I had yet to learn that no Bedu thinks it shameful to beg, and that often he will look at the gift which he has received and say, 'Is this all that you are going to give me?' I was seeing the worst side of their character, and was disillusioned and resentful, and irritated by their assumption of superiority. In consequence I was assertive and unreasonable.

Overleaf: The Rashid were among the most authentic of the Bedu, the least affected by the outside world.

It was three months before I returned to Salala. They were hard months of constant travel during which I learnt to admire my companions and to appreciate their skill. I soon found these tribesmen far easier to consort with than more progressive town Arabs who, after discarding their own customs and traditions, have adopted something of our ways. I myself infinitely preferred the Bedu's arrogant self-assurance to the Effendi's easily wounded susceptibilities. I was beginning to see the desert as the Bedu saw it, and to judge men as they judged them. I had come here looking for more than locusts, and was finding the life for which I sought.

Every man knew the individual tracks of his own camels, and some of them could remember the tracks of nearly every camel they had seen. They could tell at a glance from the depth of the footprints whether a camel was ridden or free, and whether it was in calf. By studying strange tracks they could tell the area from which the camel came. Camels from the Sands, for instance, have soft soles to their feet, marked with tattered strips of loose skin, whereas if they come from the gravel plains their feet are polished smooth. Bedu could tell the tribe to which a camel belonged, for the different tribes have different breeds of camel, all of which can be distinguished by their tracks. From looking at their droppings they could often deduce where a camel had been grazing, and they could certainly tell when it had last been watered, and from their knowledge of the country they could probably tell where. Bedu are always well informed about the politics of the desert. They know the alliances and enmities of the tribes and can guess which tribes would raid each other. No Bedu will ever miss a chance of exchanging news with anyone he meets, and he will ride far out of his way to get fresh news.

As a result of this journey I found that the country round Mughshin was suffering from many years of drought. If there had been grazing we would have found Arabs with their herds, but we had just travelled for forty-four days without seeing anyone. I asked my companions about floods and they told me that no water had reached Mughshin from the Qarra mountains since the great floods twenty-five years before. It was obviously not an 'outbreak centre' for desert locusts. I now decided to travel westwards to the Hadhramaut along the coast. No European had yet travelled in the country between Dhaufar and the Hadhramaut.

I had met with one of the Rashid sheikhs, called Musallim bin al Kamam, on my way to Mughshin, and had taken an immediate liking to him. I had asked him to meet me with some of his tribe in Salala in January, and to go with me to the Hadhramaut. I found bin al Kamam and some thirty Rashid waiting for me when I arrived at Salala on 7 January. I decided to keep Sultan and Musallim bin Tafl with me from the Bait Kathir and agreed to pay for fifteen Rashid, but bin al Kamam said that thirty men would come with us and share this pay. He explained that the country through which we should pass was frequently raided by the Yemen tribes. He had news that more than two hundred Dahm were even then raiding the Manahil on the steppes to the east of the Hadhramaut.

My ambition was to cross the Empty Quarter. I had hoped that I might be able to do so with these Rashid after we had reached the Hadhramaut, but I realized when I talked with them that by then it would be too hot. I was resolved to return, and was content to regard this first year as training for later journeys. I knew that among the Rashid I had found the Arabs for whom I was looking.

It was on this journey that I met Salim bin Kabina. He was generally known as bin Kabina, 'the son of Kabina', who was his mother. In other parts of Arabia it is common practice to call a man the son of his father; here it is more usual to use his mother's name. Bin Kabina was to be my inseparable companion during the five years I travelled in southern Arabia. He turned up while we were watering thirsty camels at a well that yielded only a few gallons an hour. For two days we worked day and night in relays. Conspicuous in a vivid red loin-cloth, and with his long hair falling round his naked shoulders, he helped us with our task. His father had died two years before and it had fallen on young bin Kabina to provide for his mother, young brother, and infant sister. I had met him at a critical moment in his life, although I only learnt this a week later.

We were walking behind the camels in the cool stillness of the early morning. Bin Kabina and I were a little apart from the others. He strode along, his body turned a little sideways as he talked, his red loin-cloth tight about his narrow hips. His rifle, held on his shoulder by its muzzle, was rusty and very ancient, and I suspected that the firing-pin was broken. He was always taking it to pieces. He told me that a month earlier he had gone down to the coast to fetch a load of sardines, and on the way back his old camel had collapsed and died. He confessed: 'I wept as I sat there in the dark beside the body of my old grey camel. She was old, long past bearing, and she was very thin for there had been no rain in the desert for a long time; but she was my camel. The only one we had. That night, Umbarak, death seemed very close to me and my family. You see, in the summer the Arabs collect round the wells; all the grazing gets eaten up for the distance of a day's journey and more; if we camped where there was grazing for the goats, how, without a camel, could we fetch water? How could we travel from one well to another?' Then he grinned at me and said, 'God brought you. Now I shall have everything.' Already I was fond of him. Attentive and cheerful, he eased the inevitable strain under which I lived, anticipating my wants. His comradeship provided a personal note in the still rather impersonal atmosphere of my desert life.

The day after we met, bin Kabina announced that he was coming with me. The Rashid sheikhs advised me to take the boy and let him look after my things. I told him he must find himself a camel and a rifle. He grinned and said that he would find both, and did. He was about sixteen years old, about five foot five in height and loosely built. He moved with a long, raking stride, like a camel, unusual among Bedu, who generally walk very upright with short steps. He was very poor, and the hardships of his life had marked him, so that his frame was gaunt and his face hollow. His hair was very long and always falling into his eyes, especially when he was cooking or otherwise busy. He would sweep it back impatiently with a thin hand. He had a rather low forehead, large eyes, a straight nose, prominent cheek-bones, and a big mouth with a long upper lip. His chin, delicately formed and rather pointed, was marked by a long scar, where he had been branded as a child to cure some illness. He had very white teeth which were always showing, for he was constantly talking and laughing.

A week later we were in the valley of the Hadhramaut and rode slowly up it to Tarim. I was interested to see this famous valley and these unspoilt Arab cities with their curious architecture. We were lavishly entertained, sitting in cushioned ease in spacious guest-rooms; we ate well-cooked food and drank water which did not taste of goatskins. My companions, however, were anxious to be gone — they fretted about their camels, which would not eat the lucerne that they were offered. I persuaded them to remain for a few days more, for I was desolate at the thought of parting with them. The privacy for which I had craved while I was with them was there behind a door, but now it was aching loneliness.

A street in Shibam: in these silent alleyways, under the sheer walls of the houses, it was like being at the bottom of a well.

The towering dwellings of Shibam stretched upwards to meet the surrounding heights.

Secret Preparations at Salala

The next year I return to Salala and make plans to cross the Empty Quarter with the help of the Rashid. I assemble a party of Bait Kathir to take me as far as Mughshin.

From Tarim I travelled to Jidda, riding a thousand miles over three months, partly on a camel and partly on a donkey, accompanied by a Sharifi boy from the Wadi al Ahsaba. Together we wandered through the Tihama, the hot coastal plain that lies between the Red Sea and the mountains, passing through villages of daub-and-wattle huts reminiscent of Africa. The people here were of uncommon beauty, and pleasantly easy and informal in their manners. We watched them, dressed in loin-cloths and with circlets of scented herbs upon their flowing hair, dancing in the moonlight to the quickening rhythm of the drums at the annual festivals when the young men were circumcised. We stayed with the Bani Hilal, destitute descendants of the most famous of all Arab tribes, in their mat shelters in the lava fields near Birk, and with the nearly naked Qahtan, who bear the name of that ancestor who sired the Arab race, and who live today in the gorges of the Wadi Baish. We visited weekly markets which sprang up at dawn in remote valleys in the mountains, or just for a day packed the streets of some small town. We saw towns of many sorts, Taif, Abha, Sabyia, and Jizan; we climbed steep passes, where baboons barked at us from the cliffs, and lammergeyer sailed out over the misty depths below. Sometimes we spent the night in a castle with an Amir, sometimes in a mud cabin with a slave, and everywhere we were well received. We fed well and slept in comfort, but I thought ceaselessly of the desert which I had left, remembering bin al Kamam, bin Kabina, Sultan, and Musallim.

Mabarak, the Sharifi boy who accompanied me during my travels through the Tihama.

As we set off from Tarim, towards Saudi Arabia, we left behind the pastoral scenes.

Amair, who had travelled with me the year before.

I arrived back in Salala on 16 October 1946. I planned to cross the Empty Quarter from Mughshin to the Trucial Coast and to return to Salala across the gravel steppes at the back of Oman.

The Bait Kathir live in the mountains and on the gravel plains to the south of the Empty Quarter. Only one section of the tribe, the Bait Musan, ever enter the Sands, and even they only know the area round Ghanim. Bertram Thomas had made his first attempt to cross the Empty Quarter with Bait Kathir and had been forced to turn back after going a short way. He had succeeded in his second attempt with the Rashid. I knew that if I were to cross the Sands I must get hold of the Rashid.

One day while buying clothes in the market I met a young Rashid, called Amair, who had been with me the year before. Until I met him I had seen no Rashid in the town and was wondering how to get in touch with them. I knew that Bait Kathir from jealousy would not be willing to help me. After I had greeted Amair I took him aside and asked him to fetch bin al Kamam, bin Kabina, and two other Rashid whom I named. I promised that I would take him with me if he found me the people I wanted. He said that bin Kabina was at Habarut, four days' journey away. He believed that bin al Kamam had gone to the Yemen to seek a truce for the Rashid with the Dahm. We arranged that he should fetch bin Kabina and meet me at Shisur in ten days' time. I was now certain that more Rashid than I required would meet me there, as indeed they did.

I left Salala on the afternoon of 25 October, with the twenty-four Bait Kathir who were to accompany me. Nearly all of them had been with me the year before. Old Tamtaim was there. I was glad that he was with me now; he would give good advice, and would keep the main party together while I was away, for I intended to cross the Sands with only a few Arabs. Sultan was also there. I knew that ultimately the decision about crossing the Sands would rest with him, and I felt confident that he would support me. He had been invaluable to me the year before. Already I was sure that he guessed my purpose, for when I commented on the poor condition of the camels he said, 'They will get us to Mughshin and we can change some of them there before we go farther.' Musallim bin Tafl was with them; while he was with us I knew that we should feed on fresh meat if there was any to be had. Mabkhaut bin Arbain was also there, and Salim bin Turkia, his kinsman, with his fifteen-year-old son, whom he wished to take with him, a handsome youth with brooding eyes and a curious cock's-comb of hair, a sign that he was still uncircumcised.

We camped at Al Ain, a spring at the foot of the Qarra mountains and spent the next day there sorting and arranging loads. I provided two thousand pounds of flour, five hundred pounds of rice, and also clarified butter, coffee, tea, sugar and some packages of poor-quality dates. There were very few dates to be had in the market at this time of year, for the dhows did not arrive with new supplies from Basra until December. I planned to be away for three months, and I intended to enlist six Rashid so that our party would number thirty-one. We had enough flour for each of us to have a daily ration of three-quarters of a pound.

We camped under some cliffs on a small level space among tumbled boulders and divided ourselves into parties of six or seven for feeding. It was difficult to move about, for the camels were couched wherever there was room for them. Many of them were being hand-fed with sardines, and the penetrating stench of the half-dried fish hung round our camp for days, until the last sardine had been eaten. The smell of decay attracted clouds of flies, which we later carried with us into the desert, clustered on our backs as we rode along. I had bought a goat for dinner, and we fed well, with boiled rice and rich savoury soup. Then Musallim brewed coffee, and Sultan produced a bowl of frothing camel's milk, warm from the udder; like all camel's milk, it tasted slightly salty. The light of the fires played over the men's bearded faces, and silhouetted the heads and necks of camels staring out into the darkness. Their eyes shone greenly. I thought of the first time I had camped here. Then I had been a stranger and lonely; now I felt that I was half accepted. I remembered the aching nostalgia for this comfortless yet satisfying life which had come over me a few months before on the slopes of the Hajaz mountains.

Old Tamtaim told me with pride that his wife had just produced a son. I remembered how after a long march he had shuffled round in a war-dance when he got off his camel, to prove that he at any rate was still as fresh as ever. I also remembered that he had once gone to sleep on his camel and fallen off, and how relieved I had been when he had got to his feet shame-faced but unhurt.

Where had I been? What had I done since I had left them? The Hajaz? Where was that? Were they Bedu there? The questions poured in, and I in turn asked others. Where was bin Lawi? Where was Bakhit bin Karaith? Had the Dahm raided the Rashid? Had any rain fallen at Mughshin? And so the hours passed, and then one by one we rose and sought a place to sleep. I had left my possessions behind a pile of rocks, near a small level spot which I had chosen, but I now found a camel couched there. I decided that there was just room for the two of us, and spread my rug and sheepskin beside her. I had brought blankets with me the year before, but, for very shame, I had given them one by one to my companions, till I was left shivering with only one. It can be very cold in the desert during the winter nights. This year I had brought a sleeping-bag. I had a few things with me but they were all that I needed. I had the clothes which I wore — a coloured loin-cloth and a long shirt that was still white but which I intended to dye russet-coloured as soon as I got into the desert and could find an *abal* bush from which to make the dye. Round my loins under my clothes I had fastened a leather cincture of many strands, such as every Bedu wears to support his back. My shirt was girded in at the waist with the belt of my heavy silver-hilted Omani dagger, so that I had a natural pocket between my shirt and skin where I could carry my compass, a small notebook, and anything else I required. I had a head-cloth from Oman, like a Kashmiri shawl, and a brown Arab cloak from the Hajaz. I had my rifle and cartridge belt. Inside my saddle-bags was spare ammunition, my camera, films, an aneroid and thermometer, a large notebook, a volume of Gibbon and *War and Peace,* a press for plants, a small medicine chest, a set of clothes for bin Kabina, since I knew that he would be in rags, the dagger which I had worn last year and which I had replaced with the one I was now wearing, and several bags of Maria Theresa dollars. These coins, dated 1780, are still minted. They are about the size of a five-shilling piece, are worth half-a-crown, and are the only coins acceptable here; the Arabs call them *riyals.*

I lay in my sleeping-bag listening to the never-ending noises. Some people were still talking. They talked at intervals through the night as, woken by the cold, they squatted around the fire. Someone else was singing quietly to himself on the far side of the camp. The camels, uncomfortable on the rocky floor, shuffled and groaned. I heard a leopard cough somewhere on the slopes above us. Others heard it too and Musallim called out, 'Did you hear that? It is a leopard.' I found it difficult to sleep; my mind was too full of plans, too stimulated by my return. I thought how welcoming are Arabs, more so than any race I know.

Two days after leaving Al Ain, we moved down to the pool of Aiyun, which lies beneath sheer-sided limestone cliffs two hundred feet in height, at the head of the Wadi Ghudun. This deep

While I was with the Arabs I wished only to live as they lived. I would gladly think that nothing in their lives was altered by my coming. Regretfully however, I realized that the maps I made helped others, with more material aims, to visit and corrupt a people whose spirit once lit the desert like a flame.

Tamtaim declared that a monster serpent lived in the pool of Aiyun and that sometimes it seized a goat when the flocks came down to drink.

pool, which is fed by a small spring, is a hundred and fifty yards long and thirty yards across, and its still, green waters are fringed with rushes.

We watered our camels and filled our water-skins. The watercourse which gave access to the pool was soon packed with jostling camels, picking their way with clumsy deliberation among the boulders and snatching mouthfuls from any bushes they passed. Musallim had gone out hunting along the cliffs, and he came in a little before sunset, carrying an ibex which he dumped down beside the fire. It was an old ram whose meat would taste much as it smelt, but it was meat. Musallim gave some to each party and then, tireless as ever, helped young bin Anauf, bin Turkia's son, to cook the rest of it.

Later he heaped the steaming rice on to a single tray, and surrounded the tray with bowls of greasy gravy. The cooked meat was set apart. Sultan then divided it into seven equal portions. Tamtaim took seven twigs and named each twig after one of us. Musallim, whose back had been turned, then placed a twig on a heap of meat, saying as he did so, 'Here is for the best man.' This lot fell to bin Turkia. 'Here is for the worst', as he laid down another twig. This was for Mabkhaut, which was not fair. 'This is for the man who won't get up in the morning.' It was mine and apposite, as the laughter reminded me, but the laughter was redoubled when Musallim called out, 'This is for the man who

pokes the girls', and Tamtaim picked up the meat which had fallen to him. Bin Anauf grinned at the old man, and said, 'Evidently, uncle, you will have another son next year.' Musallim went on until each of us had drawn his share of the meat.

After dinner we sat round and talked, the favourite occupation of the Bedu. They are unflagging talkers. A man will tell the same story half a dozen times in a couple of months to the same people and they will sit and listen with apparent interest. They find it an almost unendurable hardship to keep silent. Yet that evening when someone started to recite poetry a hush fell over the camp, broken only by the sound of pounding as they crushed *saf* leaves which they had gathered in the wadi before plaiting the fibre into rope. One after the other they gathered round, silent except when they repeated the final line of each verse.

When moved, Arabs break easily into poetry. I have heard a lad spontaneously describe in verse some grazing which he had just found: he was giving natural expression to his feelings. But while they are very sensible of the beauty of their language, they are curiously blind to natural beauty. When we returned from Mughshin the year before, and had come out from the void of the desert on to the crest of the Qarra range and looked again on green trees and grass and the loveliness of the mountains, I turned to one of them and said, 'Isn't that beautiful!' He looked, and then said uncomprehending, 'no — it is rotten bad grazing.'

The colour of the sands, a sunset, the moon reflected in the sea; such things leave the Bedu unmoved. They are not even noticed.

In this southern desert, between Oman and the Hadhramaut, there is little water. In areas as large as an English county there are only single wells, and some of these will run dry after watering a few score camels. Yet this water has to suffice for all the human beings in the area and for their stock, not only in winter when it is cool but also in summer when the temperature often reaches 115 and sometimes 120 degrees in the shade — and there is no shade. But the country was not empty. I wished it had been. Every evening our unwanted guests — sometimes a dozen, sometimes more — turned up to make further inroads on our flour.

As I rode along I reflected that nowhere in the world was there such continuity as in the Arabian desert. Here Semitic nomads, resembling my companions, must have herded their flocks before the Pyramids were built or the Flood wiped out all trace of man in the Euphrates valley. Successive civilizations rose and fell around the desert's edge: the Minaeans, Sabaeans, and Himyarites in southern Arabia; Egypt of the Pharaohs; Sumeria, Babylonia, Assyria; the Hebrews, the Phoenicians; Greeks and Romans; the Persians; the Muslim Empire of the Arabs, and finally the Turks. They lasted a few hundred or a thousand years and vanished; new races were evolved and later disappeared; religions rose and fell; men changed, adapting themselves to a changing world; but in the desert the nomad tribes lived on, the pattern of their lives but little changed over this enormous span of time.

Then, in forty years, less than a man's lifetime, all was changed; their life disintegrated. Previously the great Bedu tribes of the Najd and the Syrian desert had dominated central and northern Arabia. All traffic between the oases, villages and towns, the pilgrim caravans, everyone in fact who moved about Arabia, had to pass through the desert, and the Bedu controlled the desert. They levied tolls on travellers or looted them at will; they extorted blackmail from villagers and cultivators and from the weaker desert tribes. Bedu raiders, as elusive as the bands of Norsemen who once harried the coasts of Europe, had only to regain the desert to be free from all pursuit, whether by Roman legionaries or Turkish mercenaries.

The ascendancy of the Bedu was, however, moral as well as physical. Valuing freedom far above ease or comfort, careless of suffering, taking indeed a fierce pride in the hardship of their lives, the Bedu forced an unwilling recognition of their superiority on the villagers and townsmen who hated and affected to despise them. In the Hajaz I had heard men, sitting full-fed round the coffee hearths of great halls, disparage the Bedu as uncouth and lawless savages and curse them as infidels who neither prayed nor fasted. They had spoken scornfully of their poverty, marvelling that any human beings could endure this desert life. Then inevitably they had spoken of the Bedu's courage and their unbelievable generosity, and they had told stories, many of them fantastically improbable which they vowed were true and had recited long passages of verse about the Bani Hilal. Listening to them I had realized that the hungry ragged men whom they had just been reviling had been transmuted into the legendary heroes of the past.

The Bedu themselves never doubted their superiority. Even today such tribes as the Mutair and the Ajman would not regard it as an honour to give a girl from their tents in marriage even to the king of Arabia. I remembered asking some Rashid, who had visited Riyadh, how they had addressed the king, and they answered in surprise, 'We called him Abd al Aziz, how else would we call him except by his name?' And when I said, 'I thought you might call him Your Majesty', they answered, 'We are Bedu. We have no king but God.'

After the First World War, cars, aeroplanes, and wireless gave government for the first time in history a mobility greater than that of the Bedu. The desert was no longer a refuge for raiders but an open plain where concealment was impossible. It was a strange coincidence that at the same time as the Bedu in the Syrian desert were being brought under control with the help of modern weapons, the greatest king in Arabian history should reign in central Arabia. Abd al Aziz Ibn Saud had already broken and brought to heel the most powerful tribes in the peninsula before he introduced a single car or aeroplane into his kingdom. The peace which he had imposed would normally have disappeared with his death, and the desert would have reverted to the state of anarchy necessary to Bedu society; but I knew that the mechanical innovations which he had introduced would enable his successors to maintain the control which he had established. The desert had been pacified, and raids and tribal warfare had been effectively prevented from the Jordan valley to the northern edge of the Empty Quarter. Only here, on the far side of this great barrier of sand, did the old way of life linger on, little affected as yet by the changes in the north.

In northern and central Arabia, while the structure of tribal life was breaking down as a result of the peace which had been imposed on the tribes and of administrative interference from outside, the economy of Bedu life was also collapsing. Deprived of their inaccessibility, the tribes could no longer blackmail the government into paying them large subsidies for their good behaviour. They could no longer levy tolls on travellers, nor exact tribute from the villagers and cultivators. A man who had lost his animals from disease could no longer borrow a mount and ride forth with a raiding party to retrieve his fortune. But the most disastrous change of all was caused by the introduction of mechanical transport, which practically abolished the dependence of the townsmen and villagers on the camels which the Bedu breed. In the past the Bedu had always found a ready sale for their camels, especially the thoroughbreds, for which the Arab rulers and the richer merchants were prepared to pay large prices. Some tribes made money by carrying goods across the desert, and even where the carrying trade was in the hands of professional carriers the Bedu sold them camels and extorted tolls.

Tonight while I was warm in my sleeping-bag the others would shiver under the cold north wind. They were Bedu, and these empty spaces where there was neither shade nor shelter were their homelands. Any of them could have worked in the gardens around Salala; all of them would have scorned this easier life of lesser men. Among the Bedu only the broken are stranded among the cultivations on the desert's shore.

An elder of the Sa'ar tribe, gathered at the well at Manwakh.

The Approach to
the Empty Quarter

[
*The Rashid meet us at Shisur and we travel to Mughshin
on the edge of the Sands. An accident deprives me of all
but two of the Rashid.*

We watered at Shisur, where the ruins of a crude stone fort on a rocky mound mark the position of this famous well, the only permanent water in the central steppes.

Suddenly the sentinel on the slope above gave the alarm. We seized our rifles, which were always at hand, and took up our position round the well. The camels were quickly collected behind the mound. In the distance we could see riders approaching. In this land all strangers are counted hostile until they declare themselves. We fired two shots over their heads. They came on steadily, waving their head-cloths, and one of them jumped off his camel and threw up sand into the air. We relaxed. As they drew near, someone said, 'They are Rashid — I can see bin Shuas's camel.' Bedu can always recognize camels much farther off than they can distinguish human beings. Meeting a stranger, they can tell which tribe he belongs to by numerous signs perceptible at once to their discerning eyes: whether he wears his cartridge-belt buckled tightly or sagging low in front, whether he wears his head-cloth loosely or more closely wound round his head; the stitchings on his shirt, the folds of his loin-cloth, the leather cover in which he carries his rifle, the pattern on his saddle-bags, the way he has folded his rug above them, even the way he walks, all these reveal his identity. But above all they can tell from a man's speech to which tribe he belongs.

The riders were close now. The Bait Kathir could identify them. 'That is bin Shuas.' 'That is Mahsin.' 'That is al Auf.' 'That is bin Kabina and Amair — and Saad and bin Mautlauq.' There were seven of them, all of them Rashid. We formed up in line to receive them. They halted their camels thirty yards away, couched them by tapping them on their necks with their sticks, got off, and came towards us. Bin Shuas and bin Mautlauq wore only loin-cloths; the others were dressed in head-cloths and shirts of varying shades of brown. I recognized the tattered shirt which bin Kabina wore as the one which I had given to him when we had parted in the Hadhramaut. Only he was unarmed, without rifle or dagger. The others carried their rifles on their shoulders. Bin Shuas and al Auf had their rifles inside covers made of undressed hide and decorated with tassels. When they were a few yards away Mahsin, whom I identified by his lame leg, called out 'Salam alaikum,' and we answered together 'Alaikum as salam.' Then one behind the other they passed along our line, greeting each of us with the triple nose-kiss, nose touching nose on the right side, left side, and again on the right. They then formed up facing us. Tamtaim said to me, 'Ask their news'; but I answered 'No, you do it. You are the oldest.' Tamtaim called out, 'Your news?' Mahsin answered, 'The news is good.' Again Tamtaim asked, 'Is anyone dead? Is anyone gone?' Back came the immediate answer, 'No! Don't say such a thing.' Question and answer were as invariable as the responses in the Litany. No matter what had really happened, they never changed. They might have fought with raiders; half their party might have been killed and be lying still unburied; their camels might have been looted; any affliction might have befallen them — starvation, drought, or sickness, and still at this first formal questioning they would answer, 'The news is good.' They now returned to the camels, unsaddled them, and, after hobbling their forelegs, turned them loose. We had meanwhile spread rugs for them, and Tamtaim shouted to bin Anauf to prepare coffee. As soon as this was ready Musallim set a dish of dates before them; then, standing, he poured out coffee and handed the cup to Mahsin and to the others in their order of importance.

Al Auf's hair, very long and wavy, was unbraided and fell around his shoulders. I thought he was about thirty-five years old. He gave me an immediate impression of controlled energy, of self-confidence and intelligence.

Bin Kabina called out to me. 'How are you, Umbarak? Where have you been since you left us?' I thought he looked gaunt. He had grown an inch since I parted from him in Tarim. I was glad to see him again, for I had become much attached to him during the time he had been with me.

and kept watch across the empty, shimmering landscape, while the others finished watering the camels and filling the water-skins. Bin Kabina asked me where I was going and I told him that I planned to cross the Sands, but pledged him to secrecy for I had not yet spoken to the others. He said, 'The Bait Kathir are no good in the Sands and won't go there, but the Rashid will come with us. It is lucky that Muhammad al Auf is here, for he is the best guide in the tribe and knows the eastern Sands.' I asked him why Muhammad was nicknamed al Auf which means the Bad, and he said, 'Because he isn't.' I said, 'You are looking thin and tired. Have you been ill?' and he answered, 'I nearly died since you went away. I was circumcised three months ago and they could not stop the bleeding. When it stopped they thought it was because I was dead. There were eight of us and we were circumcised by one of the sheikhs of the Bait Khawar in the valley of the Kidyut. One of us was a Manahil, a grown man with a beard, the others were Bait Khawar. They were all older than I was. Before the operation our families rubbed our bodies with butter and saffron so that they shone. We were circumcised in turn sitting on a rock. Everyone had come to watch and there was a large crowd.' I asked him if he had been afraid, and he said, 'Of course I was.

hurt, but they don't admit it. I was most afraid that I should flinch. As I was the youngest I was done first. The old man tied my foreskin very tightly with a piece of string and then left it to die. By God it hurt! It was almost a relief when he cut it off, though his knife was blunt and he went on hacking away for what seemed ages. One of the others fainted.'

I interrupted to ask if they put anything on the wound. 'Yes,' he said, 'a mixture of salt, ashes, and powdered camel dung — it stung like fire.' He went on: 'We were operated on in the evening. I started to bleed during the night. I had been asleep and woke to feel a warm wetness on my thighs. The sheepskin on which I lay was soaked with blood. It was pitch dark and we could not see anything until my mother lit a fire. I had bled very little when they cut it off.' He added with pride, 'The people who were watching said that I showed no sign of pain while I was being done.' He told me that he had healed in three weeks, but that two of the others, one of them the Manahil with the beard, were still unhealed and very swollen when he left them two months later. When I asked why they waited till they were grown up to be operated on, he said that it was their custom, and added that some of the Mahra waited until the eve of their marriage. I wondered what effect it had on a boy to grow up

In the Tihama, the young men who were to be circumcised had danced each evening and late into the night, waiting for the day when the old men would announce that the positions of the moon and stars were favourable.

choice but to submit to it. Certainly during the operation the fear of lasting ridicule if he flinched gave him courage to endure, and his pride made him anxious to face the test. In southern Iraq I have seen fourteen- and fifteen-year-old boys thrusting each other aside as they crowded forward, as eager to be circumcised as boys to buy sweets at the counter of a school shop in England; and in the Sudan I have met Arab boys who had circumcised themselves because their fathers had delayed giving permission for the operation. Yet among Arabs, circumcision is not a coveted sign conferring special privileges and marking the emergence of a boy into manhood, as it is among many primitive tribes such as the Masai.

Bin Kabina had undergone the normal circumcision, obligatory for all Muslims, although it is usually performed on a child about the age of seven. As I sat there talking to him I thought of the ceremony I had watched five months earlier in the distant Tihama. On the appointed day, riding on camels, the initiates were paraded behind the musicians round the neighbouring villages, and then brought back just before sunset, followed by a large crowd, to their own village. Their friends helped them to take off their drawers, and then one after the other these young men, looking like girls with their flowing hair and delicate features, stepped forward in front of their tribe. Once circumcised, the lads sprang forward and, to the compelling rhythm of the drums, danced frenziedly before the eager, craning crowd, leaping and capering while the blood splashed down their legs.

The initiates wore short, tight-sleeved jackets and baggy white drawers, tight at the ankle, the only time in their lives when they wore drawers, which were women's dress.

Large mimosa-like trees, which the Arabs called ghaf, grew at the edge of the Sands. Deep down, their questing roots had found water, and their branches were heavy with flowering, trailing fronds that fell to the clean sand and formed arbours in which we camped.

We left Shisur on 9 November in the chill of dawn; the sun was resting on the desert's rim, a red ball without heat. We walked as usual till it grew warm, the camels striding in front of us, a moving mass of legs and necks. Then one by one, as the inclination took us, we climbed up their shoulders and settled in our seats for the long hours which lay ahead. The Arabs sang, 'the full-throated roaring of the tribes'; the shuffling camels quickened their pace, thrusting forward across the level ground, for we had left the hills behind us and were on the steppes which border on the Sands.

On the second day at sunset we saw the Sands stretching across our front, a shimmering rose-coloured wall, seemingly as intangible as a mirage. The Arabs, roused from the nodding torpor of weary, empty hours, pointed with their sticks, shouted, and broke into a sudden spate of talk. But I was content to look in silence upon that long-awaited vision, as excited as a mountaineer who sees above the Indian foothills the remote white challenge of the Himalayas.

We rode parallel with the Sands, since the hard gravel surface of the plain was easier for our camels than the soft steepness of the dunes. In the late afternoons we usually turned in to the Sands to camp.

We reached Mughshin eight days after leaving Shisur. We were approaching the well and Mahsin was telling us once more about the battle in which he had been wounded. His stiff leg was stretched out in front of him. Suddenly, unaccountably, our camels panicked, scattering in great plunging bounds. I saw a man fall from his camel in front of me as I fought to keep my seat. When my camel was under control I looked back.

Mahsin lay crumpled and motionless on the ground. We ran back to him. His damaged leg was twisted under him and he was moaning faintly. His head-cloth had fallen off and the close-cropped hair showed grey upon his skull. As I bent over him I realized that he was older than I had thought. We tried to straighten him but he screamed. I got morphia from my saddle-bags and gave him an injection, and then we carried him on a blanket to the trees. By the grace of God the well was close at hand. Perhaps our thirsty camels had smelt the water and this had started the stampede. We fashioned rough splints from branches and set his leg; there seemed little left but splintered bone.

In the evening we discussed what we must do. They said that Mahsin could not be moved. He must stay here till he recovered or till he died, and the Rashid must remain with him. He had killed many men, especially from the Saar, and if his enemies heard that he was lying helpless here, they would come from afar to kill him.

During the past days I had let the news leak out that I planned to cross the Empty Quarter. I knew from bin Kabina that I could count on the Rashid. Sultan and Musallim had both said they would come with me, and were insistent that I should take some of the Bait Kathir, for they were jealous of the Rashid. Now everything was changed. I was in the hands of the Bait Kathir and I wondered whether they would still be eager for this journey. Sultan soon suggested that we should travel eastwards, through the Sahma Sands where I had been the year before, and perhaps visit the quicksands of Umm al Samim which he knew I was anxious to see. I went to bed disconsolate, certain that my plans were wrecked.

Next morning bin Kabina told me that the Rashid had agreed that he and al Auf should go with me, but asked that I should lend the others two of my service rifles, and enough ammunition. I willingly agreed. Mahsin seemed better and drank a little milk. I promised him that I would remain with him till he was on the mend and I gave him another injection of morphia, for he was still in great pain. I then spoke to Sultan, hinting that as the Bait Kathir would not come with me across the Sands, I should send bin Kabina to find me more Rashid. He protested. 'Why do you speak like this, Umbarak? Listen to me! Have I not promised to take you across the Sands? I, Sultan. What do you want with the Rashid anyway. You know the Bait Kathir — old friends — your companions of last year. Did we fail you then? By God, Umbarak, why do you doubt us now?'

After incessant discussions we decided that bin Kabina, al Auf, Sultan, Musallim, Mabkhaut, bin Turkia and six other Bait Kathir should accompany me.

I remained at Mughshin for nine days. The extensive but shallow depression where the Umm al Hait ends against the Sands was well wooded with *ghaf* and tamarisk, and on the surrounding plains there were plenty of *arad* salt bushes, which are good food for camels as long as water is available.

I had a final look at Mahsin, who was much better; for several days he had refused food, but now he was eating again. Bin Shuas would be able to shoot meat for him, and one of the Rashid camels was in milk. Then we loaded up, and after saying good-bye to the others we set off into the sands. We camped a few miles away. At last I had started on my journey across the Empty Quarter.

Usually, Bedu lop tall trees to provide food for their camels, but the ghaf trees here were unmutilated, for Mughshin is a hauta where no tree may be cut. We would ride down a wadi and camp under the trees in no way remarkable from others which we had passed, but I would be warned not to damage them for this was a hauta. The Bedu believed that to ignore this prohibition would be to incur misfortune and possibly even death.

On the Edge of the Empty Quarter

[*We water for the last time at Khaur bin Atarit in Ghanim and travel to Ramlat al Ghafa.*

After our evening meal I had a long talk with Muhammad al Auf. He was the only one of our party who had been across the Sands and knew what conditions were like on the other side. The Bait Kathir were jealous of him, and he was anxious not to assume responsibility as guide until we had left the area which they knew. He said that if we could cross the formidable Uruq al Shaiba, which he described as successive mountains of sand, we should arrive at Dhafara, where in the palm groves of Liwa there were wells and villages which extended for two days' camel journey. Al Auf described Liwa to me as we sat there in the dark. It sounded very exciting. I knew that no European had ever been there, and that it must be bigger than Jabrin, which Cheesman had discovered in 1924. I asked if there was no way round these sands, and he said, 'No, only if we went far to the west by Dakaka, where Thomas crossed. There the Sands are easy'.

Bertram Thomas proved that this desert was not impassable as was once supposed. His object was to cross the Empty Quarter, and naturally he crossed it by the easiest way, where the dunes were small and the wells, known to his Rashid guides, were frequent. Philby's route had obviously been far more difficult, and the four hundred miles between wells which he covered across the western Sands at the end of his journey must always remain an epic of desert travel. Before he started from Riyadh he had heard that Thomas had already crossed from Dhaufar to Qatar. Although he was bitterly disappointed, he continued, undeterred with his plans and carried out a journey which the discerning will regard as the greater of the two. Yet Philby had certain advantages which were denied to Thomas. Once he had obtained Ibn Saud's permission to undertake the journey — and it was the king's delay in granting this permission that lost him the race — he had behind him the king's far-reaching authority. As a Muslim with the backing of the widely feared Ibn Jalawi, Governor of the Hasa, he could pass safely through the territory of the powerful Murra, whereas Thomas ran his greatest risk from this tribe, many of whom were extremely fanatical. Thomas had to make all his preparations

Al Auf reckoned that it would take us a month to get there and was worried about the Bait Kathir camels which were in poor condition. He said, 'They will never get across the Uruq al Shaiba.' Twenty waterless days was the very limit that camels would stand, travelling for long hours across heavy sands; and they would only do this if they found grazing. Should we find grazing? If we did not find it, the camels would collapse and that would be the end of us all. It is not hunger nor is it thirst that frightens the Bedu; they maintain that riding they can survive in cold weather for seven days without food or water. It is the possible collapse of their camels which haunts them.

himself. The Sultan of Muscat and his Wali in Salala were friendly, but their effective authority did not extend as far as the Qarra mountains. He discovered from experience which tribes could be of use to him, but as a Christian he was at first suspected and disliked. The measure of his achievement was that he won the confidence of these tribesmen and, with no authority behind him, persuaded them by patience and fair dealing to take him across the Sands.

I estimated that we should have to cross four hundred miles of desert before we reached Liwa. Once more we discussed camels, distances, food, and water. We were seriously short of food. We had started from Mughshin with two hundred pounds of flour, rice for two meals, one of which was eaten, a few handfuls of maize, and a little butter, coffee, sugar, and tea. This must last twelve of us for at least a month, which was half a pound of flour a day each, and nothing else. I thought bitterly of the food which the Arabs had squandered on the way to Mughshin. We should be very hungry. We could probably carry enough water for twenty days if we rationed ourselves to a quart a day for each person. I asked al Auf again what he thought; would we find grazing? 'God knows,' he answered. 'There is grazing as far as Ramlat al Ghafa from rain two years ago; beyond that, who knows?' He smiled, and added, 'We will find something.' We rose and went back to the camp to sleep, but I lay awake for a long time. The journey ahead of us seemed very formidable and I was doubtful of the Bait Kathir.

In the morning we allowed the camels to feed for a while on the *ghaf* trees which grew around our camping place. Musallim had shot a gazelle the day before, and we had eaten only half the meat. He had placed the rest in a low bush to keep it out of the sand, and when we woke it was gone. Tracks showed that a fox had taken it. I was angry, for this was the last meat we were likely to have for very many days. Musallim followed the tracks, and unearthed most of the meat where the fox had buried it under another bush. We brushed the sand off it, thankful to have recovered it.

After we had saddled we rode northward to Ghanim. This country was familiar to me, from my visit of the year before. Isolated dunes, two or three hundred feet in height, rose in apparently haphazard confusion from the desert floor. These enormous piles of sand, produced by vagaries of the winds which blew there, conform to no known rule of sand formation. The Bedu call them *qaid*. I have only seen them in the southeastern Sands and in modified form round Liwa.

We reached the well of Khaur bin Atarit on the evening of 27 November, four days after leaving Mughshin. The well was drifted in, but using our hands, and the few basins and pots which we had with us, we dug it out before nightfall. The water tasted brackish, as I had expected, and I knew that the taste would grow worse the longer we kept the water in the skins. Surprisingly it was only mildly purgative, although it contained magnesium sulphate mixed with calcium and common salt. Next day Said, the son of the Bait Musan sheikh, and two others went to look for the Bait Musan at Bir Halu, 'the sweet well'. I knew from the year before that the name was misleading; the water of Bir Halu tasted as foul as the water of Khaur bin Atarit.

I climbed to the summit of the dune and lay peacefully in the sun, four hundred feet above the well. A craving for privacy is something which Bedu will never understand; something which they will always instinctively mistrust. I have often been asked by Englishmen if I was never lonely in the desert, and have wondered how many minutes I have spent by myself in the years that I have lived there. It is true that the worst loneliness is to be lonely in a crowd. I have been lonely at school and in European towns where I knew nobody, but I have never been lonely among Arabs. I have arrived in their towns where I was unknown, and I have walked into the bazaar and greeted a shopkeeper. He has invited me to sit beside him in his shop and has sent for tea. Other people have come along and joined us. They have asked me who I was, where I came from, and innumerable questions which we should never ask a stranger. Then one of them has said, 'Come and lunch', and at lunch I have met other Arabs, and someone else has asked me to dinner.

Musallim made porridge for our evening meal, the only meal of the day. From now on we should be eating gritty lumps of unleavened bread, smeared with a little butter. We assembled to feed, and bin Kabina poured water over our outstretched hands. This was the last time we should wash, even our hands, until we reached the wells in Dhafara. Bin Kabina described the meals which he had eaten when he was with me in the Hadhramaut, probably the first time in his life that he had had enough to eat. During the months ahead we were to talk often of food, of meals which we had eaten and of others which we planned. At Mughshin my companions had spoken of women, for then they were full fed and eating meat. The Bedu are a vigorous race with strong passions, and their talk of sex is vivid and frank, but never obscene. Similarly their swearing is direct and purposeful — 'God's curse on you.' 'May God destroy your house.' 'Cursed of your two parents.' 'May raiders get you' — not the meaningless obscenities which pass for cursing among the gutter-bred Arabs of the towns. But we seldom spoke of sex, for starving men dream of food, not of women, and our bodies were too tired to lust.

The qaid are known individually to the Bedu, for each dune has its own shape; but all of them have certain features in common. Here in every case it was the northern face which was steep. On this side the sand fell away from beneath the summit in an unbroken wall, set at as steep an angle as the grains of sand would lie. On either side of this face sharp-crested ridges swept down in undulating curves, and behind them were other alternating ridges and troughs. The sand on the lower slopes at the back of the dune was firm, and rose and fell in broad sinuous trenches, or was dimpled with shallow hollows.

In the morning, we filled up some of the skins which had leaked a little and plugged the tiny dribbling holes. The Arabs said their midday prayers, and then we loaded our camels and led them away between the golden dunes. We went on foot, for the full skins were heavy on their backs. It was 29 November. We travelled north-east towards Ramlat al Ghafa, where we hoped to find the Bait Musan and to change the weakest of our camels. The going was easy, along gravel flats splashed with outcrops of white gypsum and fringed with bright-green salt-bushes. We camped at sunset, but there was nothing for our camels to eat.

The next afternoon we found a little parched herbage on the flank of a high dune. We let our camels graze for two hours and then continued until dark. Where we camped, the dunes were very big whale-backed massifs, rising above white plains of powdery gypsum. There was no warmth in this sterile scene. It was bleak and cheerless and curiously arctic in appearance. Twice I woke during the night and each time I saw Sultan brooding over the fire. We did another long day's marching, ten hours without a stop; there was nothing to stop for among these lifeless dunes. In the evening we found a little vegetation.

We started again soon after sunrise. As Sultan seemed gloomy and little inclined for conversation, I rode beside al Auf. He sat his restive, half-tamed camel with easy mastery, unconsciously anticipating her fretful movements, a confident, commanding figure, typical of a people whom no hardship can daunt.

Four hours later we came to large red dunes set close together. There were green plants growing there as the result of heavy rain which had fallen two years before. A little late we saw camels of the Bait Musan and a herdsboy who was tending them. We camped in a hollow and loosed our camels to revel among the juicy shrubs.

I climbed a slope above our camp and bin Kabina joined me. We sat there happily together, and he taught me the names of the plants which grow in the Sands. The tribulus was zahra; the heliotrope which grew on the hard sand in the hollows was rimram; and the tasselled sedge was qassis. He gave me the names of other plants and bushes: harm, the vivid green salt-bush; birkan, ailqi, sadan, and several others. He knew them all. Later when they were working out my collection in the museum in London they sometimes thought that bin Kabina had given me different names for the same plant, but nearly always, when they examined them carefully, they found that he was right.

Throughout the day my companions had gathered any plants they had seen, to feed their camels as they went along; it did not matter how high up on a dune a plant was growing, someone was sure to dismount, scramble up, and collect it. They always did this, however long or tiring the march might be.

Before setting off we gave the camels another drink. Several of them, accustomed to clean-tasting water in Dhaufar, refused to touch this bitter stuff. We held their nostrils but they still refused, and finally we had to pour it down their throats by force. It was the last water we would find till we reached Dhafara.

We bought the bull, a large and very powerful black animal, after much haggling and for a fantastic price, paying the equivalent of fifty pounds, more than twice what it was worth. I felt more confident than I had felt for days. I had with me chosen companions all mounted on good camels. We had a spare camel with us which was used to the Sands. If our food ran out we could kill one of our animals and eat it. Water was short. We should have to be careful with this, and ration ourselves to a pint a day.

Bin Kabina and I climbed a slope above the camp. There, he talked about his mother and his young brother Said, whom I had not met, and about his cousin whom he hoped to marry. Then we saw Sultan and the others returning from the Bait Musan encampment. As they drew near, bin Kabina said, 'Sultan will make trouble. He is frightened and does not wish to go on', and I knew that bin Kabina was right. They brought a bag of sour milk with them. We drank it thirstily and it was very good. Then Sultan called the others and they went off and sat in a circle apart from me. I told bin Kabina to fetch al Auf. Later Sultan asked me to join them. He said that they had discussed the situation and agreed that neither they nor our camels were capable of getting to Dhafara, that we must therefore return to the others on the southern coast. I then suggested that six of us should go on with the best of the camels, and that the other six should go back. But Sultan declared that we must either all go on or all go back. We argued for a long time but I knew that it was useless. His nerve had gone; he had lived all his life in the mountains and on the steppes. In the Sands he was confused and bewildered, no longer self-reliant. He looked an old and broken man and I was sorry. He had helped me so often and I liked him.

I asked al Auf if he would come with me, and he said: 'If you wish to go on I will guide you.' I asked bin Kabina, and he answered that where I went he would go. I wondered if Musallim would come with us. The camel which I rode belonged to him; without it I did not see how I could go on. I knew that he was jealous of Sultan. I asked him, and he answered, 'I will come.' The others said nothing.

Musallim told me that the Bait Musan possessed a bull camel in good condition, and suggested that we should buy it and take it with us as a spare. He also said that Mabkhaut bin Arbain was his friend and would come with us if he asked him to. Later Mabkhaut came over, carrying his saddlery, and joined us.

Bin Kabina, Musallim, and Mabkhaut each carried one of the service rifles which belonged to me. Al Auf had a long-barrelled ·303 Martini, a weapon favoured by the Bedu. I carried a sporting model ·303. We divided the spare ammunition between us. There was more than a hundred rounds for each of us. Next day after we had left the others, I told my companions that they could have these weapons as presents, and promised al Auf that he could take the pick of my remaining rifles as soon as we returned to Salala. Nothing that I could have given them could have delighted them more. Bin Kabina had already confided to me that he hoped to buy a rifle with the money I gave him. He no doubt had visualized himself as the proud owner of some ancient weapon, such as he had borrowed when he accompanied me to the Hadhramaut, a fighting-man at last, envied by his young brother. Now he owned the finest rifle in his tribe.

The First Crossing
of the Empty Quarter

The departure of five Bait Kathir leaves me with a party of only four. We are short of food and water. We cross the Uruq al Shaiba and arrive at Khaba well near Liwa Oasis.

The Bait Kathir helped us to load our camels. We said goodbye, picked up our rifles, and set off, passing the bush where bin Kabina and I had sat the day before. The plants he had collected to show me still lay there, withered on the ground. It seemed a long time ago.

The Rashid took the lead, their faded brown clothes harmonizing with the sands: al Auf, a lean, neat figure, very upright; bin Kabina, more loosely built, striding beside him. The two Bait Kathir followed close behind, with the spare camel tied to Musallim's saddle. Their clothes, which had once been white, had become neutral-coloured from long usage. Mabkhaut was the same build as al Auf, whom he resembled in many ways, though he was a less forceful character. In the distance he was distinguishable from him only by the colour of his shirt. Musallim, compactly built, slightly bow-legged, and physically tough, was of a different, coarser breed. The least likeable of my companions, his personality had suffered from too frequent sojourns in Salala and he tended to be ingratiating.

The following morning, bin Kabina went with one of the Bait Imani, at whose camp we had spent the night, to collect our camels, and when he came back I noticed he was no longer wearing a loin-cloth under his shirt. I asked him where it was and he said that he had given it away. I protested that he could not travel without one through the inhabited country beyond the Sands and in Oman, and that I had no other to give him. I said he must recover it and gave him some money for the man instead. He argued that he could not do this. 'What use will money be to him in the Sands. He wants a loin-cloth,' he grumbled, but at length he went off to do as I had told him.

Wishing our hosts the safe keeping of God, we turned away across the Sands. As he walked along, al Auf held out his hands, palms upwards, and recited verses from the Koran. The sand was still very cold beneath our feet. Usually, when they are in the Sands during the winter or summer, Arabs wear socks knitted from coarse black hair. None of us owned these socks and our heels were already cracking from the cold. Later these cracks became deeper and very painful. We walked for a couple of hours, and then rode till nearly sunset; encouraging our camels to snatch mouthfuls from any plants they passed. They would hasten towards each one with their lower lips flapping wildly.

Musallim rode the black bull and led his own camel, which carried the two largest water-skins. Going down a steep slope the female hesitated. The head-rope attached to the back of Musallim's saddle tightened and slowly pulled her over on to her side. I was some way behind and could see what was going to happen but there was no time to do anything. I shouted frantically at Musallim but he could not halt his mount on the slope. I prayed that the rope would break, and as I watched the camel collapse on top of the water-skins I thought, 'Now we will never get across the Sands'. Al Auf was already on the ground slashing at the taut rope with his dagger. As I jumped from my saddle I wondered if we should have even enough water left to get back to Ghanim. The fallen camel kicked out, and as the rope parted heaved herself to her knees. The water-skins which had fallen from her back still seemed to be full. Hardly daring to hope I bent over them, as al Auf said 'Praise be to God. They are all right,' and the others reiterated 'The praise be to God, the praise be to God!' We reloaded them on to the bull, which, bred in the Sands, was accustomed to these slithering descents.

At first the dunes were brick-red in colour, separate mountains of sand, rising above ash-white gypsum flats ringed with vivid green salt-bushes; those we passed in the afternoon were even higher – 500 to 550 feet in height and honey-coloured. There was little vegetation here.

When we had fed, bin Kabina took the small brass coffee-pot from the fire and served us with coffee, a few drops each. Then we crouched round the fire and talked.

I asked al Auf about his former journeys through these Sands. 'I have crossed them twice,' he said. 'The last time I came this way was two years ago. I was coming from Abu Dhabi.' I asked, 'Who was with you?' and he answered, 'I was alone.' Thinking that I must have misunderstood him, I repeated, 'Who were your companions?' 'God was my companion.' To have ridden alone through this appalling desolation was an incredible achievement. We were travelling through it now, but we carried our own world with us: a small world of five people, which yet provided each of us with companionship, with talk and laughter and the knowledge that others were there to share the hardship and the danger. I knew that if I travelled here alone the weight of this vast solitude would crush me utterly.

Later we came on some grazing and stopped for the night. We chose a hollow sheltered from the wind, unloaded the water-skins and saddle-bags, hobbled the camels, loosened the saddles on their backs and drove them off to graze.

I was happy in the company of these men who had chosen to come with me. I felt affection for them personally, and sympathy with their way of life. But though the easy equality of our relationship satisfied me, I did not delude myself that I could be one of them. They were Bedu and I was not; they were Muslims and I was a Christian. Nevertheless, I was their companion and an inviolable bond united us, as sacred as the bond between host and guest, transcending tribal and family loyalties. Because I was their companion on the road, they would fight in my defence even against their brothers and they would expect me to do the same.

But I knew that for me the hardest test would be to live with them in harmony and not to let my impatience master me; neither to withdraw into myself, nor to become critical of standards and ways of life different from my own. I knew from experience that the conditions under which we lived would slowly wear me down, mentally if not physically, and that I should be often provoked and irritated by my companions. I also knew with equal certainty that when this happened the fault would be mine, not theirs.

At dawn al Auf untied the camels, which he had brought in for the night, and turned them loose to graze. There would be no food till sunset, but bin Kabina heated what was left of the coffee. After we had travelled for an hour we came upon a patch of grazing freshened by a recent shower. Faced with the choice of pushing on or of feeding the camels al Auf decided to stop, and as we unloaded them he told us to collect bundles of tribulus to carry with us.

At midday we went on, passing high, pale-coloured dunes, and others that were golden, and in the evening we wasted an hour skirting a great mountain of red sand, probably 650 feet in height. Beyond it we travelled along a salt-flat, which formed a corridor through the Sands. Looking back I fancied the great, red dune was a door which was slowly, silently closing behind us. I watched the narrowing gap between it and the dune on the other side of the corridor, and imagined that once it was shut we could never go back, whatever happened. The gap vanished and now I could see only a wall of sand. I turned back to the others and they were discussing the price of a coloured loin-cloth which Mabkhaut had bought in Salala before we started. Suddenly al Auf pointed to a camel's track and said, 'Those were made by my camel when I came this way on my way to Ghanim.'

We stopped at sunset for the evening meal, and fed to our camels the tribulus we had brought with us. All the skins were sweating and we were worried about our water. There had been a regular and ominous drip from them throughout the day, a drop falling on to the sand every few yards as we rode along, like blood dripping from a wound that could not be staunched. There was nothing to do but to press on, and yet to push the camels too hard would be to founder them. They were already showing signs of thirst. Al Auf had decided to go on again after we had fed.

Bin Kabina, some camel fodder in his hands, near the summit on the windward and easy side of a great dune. The sharp ridge is formed by occasional winds from the opposite direction.

After the meal we rode for two hours along a salt-flat. The dunes on either side, colourless in the moonlight, seemed higher by night than by day. The lighted slopes looked very smooth, the shadows in their folds inky black. Soon I was shivering uncontrollably from the cold. The others roared out their songs into a silence, broken otherwise only by the crunch of salt beneath the camels' feet. Eventually we halted and I dismounted numbly. I would have given much for a hot drink but I knew that I must wait eighteen hours for that. We lit a small fire and warmed ourselves before we slept, though I slept little. I was tired; for days I had ridden long hours on a rough camel, my body racked by its uneven gait. I suppose I was weak from hunger, for the food which we ate was a starvation ration, even by Bedu standards. But my thirst troubled me most; it was not bad enough really to distress me but I was always conscious of it. Even when I was asleep I dreamt of racing streams of ice-cold water, but it was difficult to get to sleep. Now I lay there trying to estimate the distance we had covered and the distance that still lay ahead. When I had asked al Auf how far it was to the well, he had answered, 'It is not the distance but the great dunes of the Uruq al Shaiba that may destroy us.'

The others were awake at the first light, anxious to push on while it was still cold. The camels sniffed at the withered tribulus but were too thirsty to eat it. In a few minutes we were ready. We plodded along in silence. My eyes watered with the cold; the jagged salt-crusts cut and stung my feet. The world was grey and dreary. Then gradually the peaks ahead of us stood out against a paling sky; almost imperceptibly they began to glow, borrowing the colours of the sunrise which touched their crests.

Al Auf told us to wait while he went to reconnoitre. I watched him walking away across the glistening salt-flat, his rifle on his shoulder and his head thrown back as he scanned the slopes above. He looked superbly confident, but as I viewed this wall of sand I despaired that we would ever get the camels up it. Mabkhaut evidently thought the same, for he said to Musallim, 'We will have to find a way round. No camel will ever climb that.' Musallim answered, 'It is al Auf's doing. He brought us here. We should have gone much farther to the west, nearer to Dakaka.'

I went over to a bank and sat down to wait for al Auf's return. The ground was still cold, although the sun was now well up, throwing a hard, clear light on the barrier of sand ahead of us. It seemed fantastic that this great rampart which shut out half the sky could be made of wind-blown sand. Now I could see al Auf, about half a mile away, moving along the salt-flat at the bottom of the dune. While I watched him he started to climb a ridge, like a mountaineer struggling upward through soft snow towards a pass over a high mountain. I even saw the tracks which he left behind him. He was the only moving thing in all that empty, silent landscape.

Overleaf: A high unbroken dune-chain stretched across our front. It was not of uniform height, but, like a mountain range, consisted of peaks and connecting passes. Several of the summits appeared to be seven hundred feet above the salt-flat on which we stood.

What were we going to do if we could not get the camels over it? I knew that we could not go any farther to the east, for al Auf had told me that the quicksands of Umm al Samim were in that direction. To the west the easier Sands of Dakaka, where Thomas had crossed, were more than two hundred miles away. We had no margin, and could not afford to lengthen our journey. Our water was already dangerously short, and even more urgent than our own needs were those of the camels, which would collapse unless they were watered soon. We must get them over this monstrous dune, if necessary by unloading them and carrying the loads to the top. But what was on the other side? How many more of these dunes were there ahead of us? If we turned back now we might reach Mughshin, but I knew that once we crossed this dune the camels would be too tired and thirsty to get back even to Ghanim. Then I thought of Sultan and the others who had deserted us, and of their triumph if we gave up and returned defeated. Looking again at the dune ahead I noticed that al Auf was coming back. A shadow fell across the sand beside me. I glanced up and bin Kabina stood there. He smiled, said 'Salam alaikum', and sat down. Urgently I turned to him and asked, 'Will we ever get the camels over that?' He pushed the hair back from his forehead, looked thoughtfully at the slopes above us, and answered, 'It is very steep but al Auf will find a way. He is a Rashid; he is not like these Bait Kathir.' Unconcernedly he then took the bolt out of his rifle and began to clean it with the hem of his shirt, while he asked me if all the English used the same kind of rifle.

When al Auf approached we went over to the others. Mabkhaut's camel had lain down; the rest of them stood where we had left them, which was a bad sign. Ordinarily they would have roamed off at once to look for food. Al Auf smiled at me as he came up but said nothing, and no one questioned him. Noticing that my camel's load was unbalanced he heaved up the saddle-bag from one side, and then picking up with his toes the camel-stick which he had dropped, he went over to his own camel, caught hold of its head-rope, said 'Come on', and led us forward.

It was now that he really showed his skill. He picked his way unerringly, choosing the inclines up which the camels could climb. Here on the lee side of this range a succession of great faces flowed down in unruffled sheets of sand, from the top to the very bottom of the dune. They were unscalable, for the sand was poised always on the verge of avalanching, but they were flanked by ridges where the sand was firmer and the inclines easier. It was possible to force a circuitous way up these slopes, but not all were practicable for camels, and from below it was difficult to judge their steepness. Somehow we reached the top. Before slumping down on the sand I looked anxiously ahead of us. To my relief I saw that we were on the edge of rolling downs, where the going would be easy among shallow valleys and low, rounded hills. 'We have made it. We are on top of Uruq al Shaiba', I thought triumphantly. The fear of this great obstacle had lain like a shadow on my mind ever since al Auf had first warned me of it, the night we spoke together in the Sands of Ghanim. Now the shadow had lifted and I was confident of success.

We rested for a while on the sand, not troubling to talk, until al Auf rose to his feet and said 'Come on'. Some small dunes built up by cross-winds ran in curves parallel with the main face across the back of these downs.

We mounted our camels. My companions had muffled their faces in their head-cloths and rode in silence, swaying to the camels' stride. The shadows on the sand were very blue, of the same tone as the sky; two ravens flew northward, croaking as they passed. I struggled to keep awake. The only sound was made by the slap of the camels' feet, like wavelets lapping on a beach.

Very slowly, a foot at a time, we coaxed the unwilling beasts upward. Each time we stopped I looked up at the crests where the rising wind was blowing streamers of sand into the void, and wondered how we should ever reach the top.

The steep faces of smaller dunes were to the north and the camels slithered down them without difficulty. These downs were brick-red splashed with deeper shades of colour.

To rest the camels we stopped for four hours in the late after-noon on a long gentle slope which stretched down to another salt-flat. There was no vegetation on it and no salt-bushes bordered the plain below us. Al Auf announced that we would go on again at sunset. While we were feeding I said to him cheerfully, 'Anyway, the worst should be over now that we are across the Uruq al Shaiba.' He looked at me for a moment and then answered, 'If we go well tonight we should reach them tomorrow.' I said, 'Reach what?' and he replied, 'The Uruq al Shaiba', adding, 'Did you think what we crossed today was the Uruq al Shaiba? That was only a dune. You will see them tomorrow.' For a moment, I thought he was joking, and then I realized that he was serious, that the worst of the journey which I had thought was behind us was still ahead. We went on until midnight.

Al Auf woke us again while it was still dark. As usual bin Kabina made coffee, and the sharp-tasting drops which he poured out stimulated but did not warm. The grunting camels heaved themselves erect. We lingered for a moment more beside the fire; then al Auf said 'Come', and we moved forward. Beneath my feet the gritty sand was cold as frozen snow.

We were faced by a range as high as, perhaps even higher than, the range we had crossed the day before, but here the peaks were steeper and more pronounced, rising in many cases to great pinnacles, down which the flowing ridges swept like draperies. These sands, paler coloured than those we had crossed, were very soft, cascading round our feet as the camels struggled up the slopes. We led the trembling, hesitating animals upward along great sweeping ridges where the knife-edged crests crumbled beneath our feet. Although it was killing work, my companions were always gentle and infinitely patient. The sun was scorching hot and I felt empty, sick, and dizzy. As I struggled up the slope, knee-deep in shifting sand, my heart thumped wildly and my thirst grew worse. I found it difficult to swallow; even my ears felt blocked, and yet I knew that it would be many intolerable hours before I could drink. I would stop to rest, dropping down on the scorching sand, and immediately it seemed I would hear the others shouting, 'Umbarak, Umbarak'; their voices sounded strained and hoarse. It took us three hours to cross this range.

On the summit were no gently undulating downs such as we had met the day before. Instead, three smaller dune-chains rode upon its back, and beyond them the sand fell away to a salt-flat in another great empty trough between the mountains. The range on the far side seemed even higher than the one on which we stood, and behind it were others. I looked round, seeking instinctively for some escape. There was no limit to my vision. Somewhere in the ultimate distance the sands merged into the sky, but in that infinity of space I could see no living thing, not even a withered plant to give me hope. 'There is nowhere to go', I thought. 'We cannot go back and our camels will never get up another of these awful dunes. We really are finished.' The silence flowed over me, drowning the voices of my companions and the fidgeting of their camels.

We went down into the valley, and somehow — and I shall never know how the camels did it — we got up the other side. There, utterly exhausted, we collapsed. Al Auf gave us each a little water, enough to wet our mouths. He said, 'We need this if we are to go on.' The midday sun had drained the colour from the sands. Scattered banks of cumulus cloud threw shadows across the dunes and salt-flats, and added an illusion that we were high among Alpine peaks, with frozen lakes of blue and green in the valley, far below. Half asleep, I turned over, but the sand burnt through my shirt and woke me from my dreams.

I wondered how much more these camels would stand, for they were trembling violently whenever they halted. When one refused to go on we heaved on her head-rope, pushed her from behind, and lifted the loads on either side as we manhandled the roaring animal upward. Sometimes one of them lay down and refused to rise, and then we had to unload her, and carry the water-skins and the saddlebags ourselves. Not that the loads were heavy. We had only a few gallons of water left and some handfuls of flour.

It was midnight when at last Al Auf said, 'Let's stop here. We will get some sleep and give the camels a rest. The Uruq al Shaiba are not far away now.' In my dreams that night they towered above us higher than the Himalayas.

Two hours later al Auf roused us. As he helped me load my camel, he said, 'Cheer up, Umbarak. This time we really are across the Uruq al Shaiba', and when I pointed to the ranges ahead of us, he answered, 'I can find a way through those; we need not cross them.' We went on till sunset, but we were going with the grain of the country, following the valleys and no longer trying to climb the dunes. We should not have been able to cross another. There was a little fresh *qassis* on the slope where we halted. I hoped that this lucky find would give us an excuse to stop here for the night, but, after we had fed, al Auf went to fetch the camels, saying, 'We must go on again while it is cool if we are ever to reach Dhafara.'

We stopped long after midnight and started again at dawn, still exhausted from the strain and long hours of yesterday, but al Auf encouraged us by saying that the worst was over. The dunes were certainly lower than they had been, more uniform in height and more rounded, with fewer peaks. Four hours after we had started we came to rolling uplands of gold and silver sand, but still there was nothing for the camels to eat. A hare jumped out from under a bush, and al Auf knocked it over with his stick. The others shouted 'God has given us meat.' For days we had talked of food; every conversation seemed to lead back to it. Since we had left Ghanim I had been always conscious of the dull ache of hunger, yet in the evening my throat was dry even after my drink, so that I found it difficult to swallow the dry bread Musallim set before us.

We were across the Uruq al Shaiba and intended to celebrate our achievement with this gift from God. Unless our camels foundered we were safe; even if our water ran out we should live to reach a well.

We started very early the next morning and rode without a stop for seven hours across easy rolling downs. The colour of these sands was vivid, varied, and unexpected: in places the colour of ground coffee, elsewhere brick-red, or purple, or a curious golden-green. There were small white gypsum-flats, fringed with *shanan*, a grey-green salt-bush, lying in hollows in the downs. We rested for two hours on sands the colour of dried blood and then led our camels on again.

We started again in the late afternoon after having met Hamad, a Sheikh of the Rashid, and travelled till sunset. Hamad came with us and said he would stay with us until we had got food from Liwa. Knowing where the Arabs were encamped he could help us to avoid them, so that news of my presence would not get about among the tribes. Next day, after seven hours'

travelling, we reached Khaur Sabakha on the edge of the Dhafara Sands. We cleaned out the well and found brackish water at seven feet, so bitter that even the camels only drank a little before refusing it. They sniffed thirstily at the water with which al Auf tried to coax them from a leather bucket, but only dipped their lips into it. We covered their noses but still they would not drink.

The next day when we halted in the afternoon al Auf told us we had reached Dhafara and that Khaba well was close. He said that he would fetch water in the morning. We finished what little was left in one of our skins. Next day we remained where we were. Hamad said that he would go for news and return the following day. Al Auf, who went with him, came back in the afternoon with two skins full of water which, although slightly brackish, was delicious after the filthy evil-smelling dregs we had drunk the night before.

It was 12 December, fourteen days since we had left Khaur bin Atarit in Ghanim.

In the evening, now that we needed no longer measure out each cup of water, bin Kabina made extra coffee, while Musallim increased our rations of flour by a mugful. This was wild extravagance, but we felt that the occasion called for celebration. Even so, the loaves he handed us were woefully inadequate to stay our hunger, now that our thirst was gone.

For years the Empty Quarter had represented to me the final, unattainable challenge which the desert offered. Suddenly it had come within my reach. I remembered my excitement when Lean had casually offered me the chance to go there, the immediate determination to cross it, and then the doubts and fears, the frustrations, and the moments of despair. Now I had crossed it. To others my journey would have little importance. It would produce nothing except a rather inaccurate map which no-one was ever likely to use. It was a personal experience, and the reward had been a drink of clean, nearly tasteless water. I was content with that.

On the edge of the Dhafara Sands.

Looking back on the journey I realized that there had been no high moment of achievement such as a mountaineer must feel when he stands upon his chosen summit. Over the past days new strains and anxieties had built up as others eased, for, after all, this crossing of the Empty Quarter was set in the framework of a longer journey, and already my mind was busy with the new problems which our return journey presented.

Return to Salala

[
To avoid crossing more sand we return over the gravel plains of Oman, a long detour made difficult by the distrust of the tribes and our lack of food.

The dunes ran from west to east so that we were travelling easily.

We were across the Empty Quarter, but we still had to return to Salala. We could not go back the way we had come. The only possible route was through Oman.

I tried to work out our position on a map which showed Mughshin and Abu Dhabi but nothing else, except from hearsay. It was difficult to plot our course with no firm surface larger than my notebook on which to work. Bin Kabina held the map while the others sat and watched, and all of them distracted me with questions. They could never follow a map unless it was orientated, though curiously enough they could understand a photograph even when they held it upside down. I estimated that we should have between five hundred and six hundred miles to travel before we could rejoin Tamtaim and the rest of the Bait Kathir on the southern coast, and then a further two hundred miles to reach Salala. I asked al Auf about water and he said, 'Don't worry about that, there are plenty of wells ahead of us. It is food which is going to be our trouble.' We went over to the saddle-bags and Musallim measured out the flour. There were nine mugfuls left — about seven pounds.

Hamad assured us that we should be able to buy plenty of food in Liwa, enlarging on what we should find there — flour and rice and dates and coffee and sugar — but he added that it would take us three, perhaps four, days to get there. I said wryly, 'We shall be as hungry as the camels', and al Auf grunted, 'Yes, but the sons of Adam cannot endure like camels.' Hamad, questioned by Mabkhaut and Mussalim, said that as long as we remained to the south of Liwa we should be outside the range of the fighting on the coast, and insisted that all the tribes in the south, whether they were Awamir, Manasir, or Bani Yas, were on good terms with the Rashid. He said, 'It will be different when you reach Oman. There the Duru are our enemies. There is no good in any of the Duru. You will have to be careful while you are among them for they are a treacherous race.' Al Auf laughed and quoted, 'He died of snake-bite', a well-known expression for Duru treachery. He then said thoughtfully, 'The difficulty is Umbarak. No one must know he is here. If the Arabs hear there

My companions had wrapped themselves in their cloaks and muffled their faces in their head-cloths till only their eyes showed. Arabs argue that the extra clothes which they put on when it is hot keep the heat out; in fact, what they do is stop the sweat from evaporating and thereby build up a cool layer of air next to the skin. I could never bear this clammy discomfort and preferred to lose moisture by letting the hot air dry my skin. But if I had done this in summer I should have died of heat-stroke.

is a Christian in the Sands they will talk of nothing else. We don't want the news about Umbarak to get ahead of us among the Duru. If we meet any Arabs we had better say that we are Rashid from the Hadhramaut, travelling to Abu Dhabi to fight for the Al bu Falah. Umbarak can be an Arab from Aden.' Turning to me, he said, 'From now on you must ride all the time. Any Arab who came across your monstrous footprints would certainly follow them to find out who on earth you were.' He got up to fetch the camel, saying, 'We had better be off.'

We went down to Khaba well, three miles away in a bare hollow, among a jumble of small, white crescent-dunes. The water was ten feet below the surface, and it took us a long time to water the camels, for we had only one small leather bucket, and each camel drank ten to twelve gallons. At last all of them were satisfied, blown out with the water which they had sucked up in long slow draughts. Al Auf dashed a few bucketfuls against their chests, and then started to fill the water-skins. The sun was very hot before we had finished. We mounted.

Three days after leaving Khaba we reached the Batin, and lay up in the dunes near Balagh well. Next morning Hamad, Jadid, another Rashid, and bin Kabina went to the settlements in Liwa to buy food. They took three camels with them, and I told bin Kabina to buy flour, sugar, tea, coffee, butter, dates, and rice if he could get any, and above all to bring back a goat. Our flour was finished, but that evening Musallim produced from his saddle-bags a few handfuls of maize, which we roasted and ate. It was to be the last food we had until the others returned three days later. They were three interminable nights and days.

I had almost persuaded myself that I was conditioned to starvation, indifferent to it. After all, I had been hungry for weeks, and even when we had had flour I had had little inclination to eat the charred or sodden lumps which Musallim had cooked. I used to swallow my portion with even less satisfaction than that with which I eventually voided it. Certainly I thought and talked incessantly of food, but as a prisoner talks of freedom, for I realized that the joints of meat, the piles of rice, and the bowls of steaming gravy which tantalized me could have no reality outside my mind. I had never thought then that I should dream of the crusts which I was rejecting.

For the first day my hunger was only a more insistent feeling of familiar emptiness; something which, like a toothache, I could partly overcome by an effort of will. I woke in the grey dawn craving for food, but by lying on my stomach and pressing down I could achieve a semblance of relief. At least I was warm. Later, as the sun rose, the heat forced me out of my sleeping-bag. I threw my cloak over a bush and lay in the shade and tried to sleep again. I dozed and dreamt of food; I woke and thought of food. I tried to read, but it was difficult to concentrate. A moment's slackness and I was thinking once more of food. I filled myself with water, and the bitter water, which I did not want, made me feel sick. Eventually it was evening and we gathered round the fire, repeating, 'Tomorrow they will be back'; and thought of the supplies of food which bin Kabina would bring with him, and of the goat which we should eat. But the next day dragged out till sunset, and they did not come.

On the third morning I watched Mabkhaut turn the camels out to graze, and as they shuffled off, spared for a while from the toil which we imposed upon them, I found that I could only think of them as food. I was glad when they were out of sight. Al Auf came over and lay down near me, covering himself with his cloak; I don't think we spoke. I lay with my eyes shut, insisting to myself, 'If I were in London I would give anything to be here.' Then I thought of the jeeps and lorries with which the Locust Officers in the Najd were equipped. So vivid were my thoughts that I could hear the engines, smell the stink of petrol fumes. No, I would rather be here starving as I was than sitting in a chair, replete with food, listening to the wireless, and dependent upon cars to take me through Arabia. I clung desperately to this conviction. It seemed infinitely important. Even to doubt it was to admit defeat, to forswear everything to which I held.

The sun had set and we had given up hope when they returned. I saw at once that they had no goat with them. My dream of a large hot stew vanished. We exchanged the formal greetings and asked the formal questions about the news. Then we helped them with the only camel which was loaded. Bin Kabina said wearily, 'We got nothing. There is nothing to be had

I asked bin Kabina about Liwa. He said: 'There are palms, good ones, and quite a lot of them on the dunes above the salt-flats. The houses are of mats and palm fronds. I never saw a mud house.'

in Liwa. We have two packages of bad dates and a little wheat. They would not take our *riyals* — they wanted rupees. At last they took them at the same valuation as rupees, God's curse on them!' He had run a long palm-splinter into his foot and was limping. I tried to get it out but it was already too dark to see.

We opened a package of dates and ate. They were of poor quality and coated with sand, but there were plenty of them. Later we made porridge from the wheat, squeezing some dates into it to give it a flavour. After we had fed, al Auf said, 'If this is all we are going to have we shall soon be too weak to get on our camels.' We were a depressed and ill-tempered party that evening.

We had to get back across Arabia, travelling secretly, and we had enough food for ten days if we were economical. I had eaten tonight, but I was starving. I wondered how much longer I should be able to face this fare. We must get more food. Al Auf said, 'We must get hold of a camel and eat that', and I thought of living for a month on sun-dried camel's meat and nothing else. Hamad suggested that we should lie up near Ibri in the Wadi al Ain, and send a party into Ibri to buy food. He said, 'It is one of the biggest towns in Oman. You will get everything you want there.' With difficulty I refrained from pointing out that he had said this of Liwa.

Musallim interrupted and said that we could not possibly go into the Duru country. Al Auf asked him impatiently where in that case he did propose to go. I joined in and reminded Musallim that we had always planned to return through the Duru country.

Eventually we agreed that we must get food from Ibri and that meanwhile we would buy a camel from the Rashid who were ahead of us in the Rabadh. Hamad said, 'You must conceal the fact that Umbarak is a Christian.' Mabkhaut suggested that I should pretend that I was a *saiyid* from the Hadhramaut, since no-one would ever mistake me for a Bedu. I protested, 'That is no good; as a *saiyid* I should get involved in religious discussions. A nice mess I should make of that.' The others laughed and agreed that this suggestion would not work. I said, 'While we are in the Sands here I had better be an Aden townsman who has been living with the tribes and is now on his way to Abu Dhabi. When we get to Oman I will say I am a Syrian who has been visiting Riyadh and that I am now on my way to Salala.' Bin Kabina asked, 'What is a Syrian?' and I said, 'If you don't know what a Syrian is I don't suppose the Duru will either. Certainly they will never have seen one.'

Hamad now volunteered to accompany us as far as Ibri, since he knew the Sands and the present distribution of the tribes. He said that we had better keep along the southern edge of Liwa, where the country was at present empty.

In the morning, we ate some dates, and set off in an easterly direction, the mist still thick about us. I hoped we should not stumble on some Arab encampment. The mist did not lift for another two hours.

Huaishil, a sheikh of the Duru. Back in Mughshin, Sultan had told me that the Duru, after hearing I had visited Mughshin last year, had vowed that they would allow no infidel to travel in their country.

The dunes ran from west to east so that we were travelling easily. They consisted of great massifs similar to the *qaid* which I had seen in Ghanim, but there they were linked together to form parallel dune chains about three hundred feet in height, the broad valleys between them being covered with bright-green salt-bushes. We passed several palm groves and a few small settlements of dilapidated huts made, as bin Kabina had described, from matting and palm fronds. They were all abandoned.

We travelled slowly to rest our camels and reached the Rabadh Sands five days after leaving Balagh. Sometimes we saw camels. We would ride over to them, for travellers in the desert may milk any camels they encounter. On one occasion we came upon a small encampment of Manasir. Hamad insisted that we must go over to them, or we should arouse their suspicions since they had already seen us. I suggested that they should leave the camels to graze and that I should herd them until they returned. After some argument they agreed. I knew that they wanted milk, and I should have liked a drink myself, but it seemed stupid to run the risk of detection. When they returned, bin Kabina grinned whenever he looked at me, so I asked him what the joke was. He said, 'The Manasir gave us milk but insisted that we should fetch you, saying, "Why do you leave your companion without milk?" Al Auf explained that you were our slave, but they still insisted that we should fetch you.' I knew that among Bedu even a slave is considered as a travelling companion, entitled to the same treatment as the rest of the party. Bin Kabina went on, 'Finally al Auf said, "Oh! he is half-witted. Leave him where he is"', and the Manasir insisted no more.' Mabkhaut said, 'True, they said no more, but they looked at us a bit oddly.'

Near Rabadh, Musallim suddenly jumped off his camel, pushed his arm into a shallow burrow, and pulled out a hare. I asked him how he knew it was there, and he said that he had seen its track going in and none coming out. The afternoon dragged on until we reached the expanse of small contiguous dunes which give these sands the name of Rabadh. There was adequate grazing, so we stopped on their edge. We decided to eat the rest of our flour, and Musallim conjured three onions and some spices out of his saddle-bags. We sat round in a hungry circle watching bin Kabina cooking the hare, and offering advice. Anticipation mounted, for it was more than a month since we had eaten meat, except for the hare that al Auf had killed near the Uruq al Shaiba. We sampled the soup and decided to let it stew just a little longer. Then bin Kabina looked up and groaned, 'God! Guests!'

Coming across the sands towards us were three Arabs. Hamad said, 'They are Bakhit, and Umbarak, and Salim, the children of Mia', and to me, 'They are Rashid.' We greeted them, asked the news, made coffee for them, and then Musallim and bin Kabina dished up the hare and the bread for them, saying with every appearance of sincerity that they were our guests, that God had brought them, and that today was a blessed day. They asked us to join them but we refused, repeating that they were our guests. I hoped that I did not look as murderous as I felt while I joined the others in assuring them that God had brought them on this auspicious occasion. When they had finished, bin Kabina put a sticky lump of dates in a dish and called us over to feed.

The Arabs describe the singing of the sands as roaring, which is perhaps a more descriptive word. During the five years that I was in these parts I only heard it half a dozen times. It is caused, I think, by one layer of sand slipping over another. Once I was standing on a dunecrest and the sound started as soon as I stepped on to the steep face.

Two days later we saw some tents, and Hamad said, 'I don't know who they are', so we bore off to the right in order to pass wide of them; but a man came out from among them and ran across the sand towards us, shouting, 'Stop! Stop!' As he came near, Hamad said, 'It is all right. He is Salim, old Muhammad's son.' We greeted him and he said, 'Why do you pass by my tent? Come, I will give you fat and meat.' I protested instinctively, but he silenced me by saying, 'If you do not come to my tent I shall divorce my wife.' This was the divorce oath, which he was bound to obey if we refused. He took my camel's rein and led her towards the tents. An old man came forward and greeted us. Hamad said, 'This is old Muhammad.' Salim called to al Auf and together they went off across the dunes. They came back later with a young camel, which they slaughtered behind the tents.

Meanwhile the old man had made coffee and set out dates for us to eat. Hamad said, 'He is the Christian.' The old man asked, 'Is he the Christian who travelled last year with bin al Kamam and the Rashid to the Hadhramaut?' and after Hamad had assented he turned to me and said, 'A thousand welcomes.' It had not taken long for this news to arrive, although here we were near the Arabian Gulf, far from the Hadhramaut; but I was not surprised. I knew how interested Bedu always are in 'the news', how concerned to get the latest information about their kinsmen, about raids and tribal movements and grazing. I knew from experience how far they would go out of their way to ask for news.

It was late in the afternoon when Salim spread a rug in front of us, and placed on it a large tray covered with rice. He lifted joints of meat from the cauldron and put them on this, ladled soup over the rice, and finally tipped a dishful of butter over it. He then poured water over our outstretched hands. Gorged at last, we licked our fingers and rose together muttering 'God requite you.' We washed, using water. There was no need here to clean our fingers with sand, for the well was near by. Salim then handed us coffee and the bitter drops were welcome and clean-tasting after the greasy rice and cold lumps of fat which we had eaten. He and his father urged us to remain with them at least for another day to rest ourselves and our camels, and we willingly agreed. They brought us milk at sunset and we drank till we could drink no more. As each of us handed back the bowl from which he had drunk, he said, 'God bless her!', a blessing on the camel who had given the milk. Bakhit and Umbarak turned up next morning, saying that they had expected to find us here. Bakhit was anxious to accompany us to Ibri, where he wished to buy rice and coffee with the money we had given him for the camel. He was afraid to go alone because of the enmity between the Rashid and the Duru.

To travel safely among the Duru we needed a *rabia* or companion, who could frank us through their territory. He could be either from the Duru or from some other tribe entitled by tribal custom to give his travelling companions protection among the Duru while they were in his company. A *rabia* took an oath: 'You are my companions and your safety, both of your blood and of your possessions, is in my face.' Members of the same party were responsible for each other's safety, and were expected to fight if necessary in each other's defence, even against their own tribes or families. If one of the party was killed, all the party were involved in the ensuing blood-feud. No tribe would be likely to attack a party which was accompanied by a tribesman from a powerful tribe to which they were allied, but a *rabia* could belong to a small and insignificant tribe and still give protection. The question of how and where each tribe could give protection was complicated. Our present difficulty was that we should have to penetrate into the Duru territory without a *rabia* and hope to find one when we arrived there. At present the Rashid and the Duru were not at war, but there was no love lost between them.

Three days later we camped on the eastern edge of the Sands among some scattered thorn-bushes, and the following day we rode for seven hours across a flat plain, whose gravel surface was overspread with fragments of limestone. Ahead of us a yellow haze hung like a dirty curtain across the horizon. We camped in the evening in a sandy watercourse, among some *ghaf* trees. There was a large package of dates in the fork of one of these, left there by its owner in perfect confidence that no one would touch it. At sunset we saw some goats in the distance; but no-one came near us. During the night a wolf howled round our camp; it was one of the eeriest sounds I have ever heard.

Muhammad, Salim's father, had a long white beard kindly eyes, and a gentle voice. He walked very upright, as do all the Bedu.

Old Muhammad invited us to eat, but refused our invitation to join us. He stood and watched us, saying, 'Eat! Eat! You are hungry. You are tired. You have come a long way. Eat!' He shouted to Salim to bring more butter, although we protested that there was enough already, and taking the dish from Salim's hand poured it over the rice.

From our camp I could see the long range of Jabal al Akhadar (on the extreme right here, behind Jabal Kaur), the Green Mountain, which lies behind Muscat. It rises to ten thousand feet and was still unexplored. I could see other and nearer mountains, none of which were marked on my map. What was shown was guesswork. The Wadi al Ain, for instance, was marked as flowing into the sea near Abu Dhabi. I was more than ever determined to come back and explore this country properly.

At dawn I saw a great mountain to the east and Hamad told me that it was Jabal Kaur near Ibri. As we approached the Wadi al Ain, Hamad suggested that he and al Auf had better ride on ahead, in case there was anyone on the well, so that they could give them warning of our approach; otherwise they would certainly shoot at us. They trotted off towards the belt of trees which stretched across our front. A little later, when we arrived near the well, we saw a group of Arabs arguing with Hamad; al Auf came to us and told us to stop where we were as there was trouble. Hurriedly he explained that when they had reached the well they spoke to two Duru who were watering camels, and that these men had been friendly, but that some other Duru, with camels loaded with dates from Ibri, had arrived shortly afterwards and they had declared that no Rashid might use their well. Al Auf then went back to the group round the well, while we waited anxiously to see what was going to happen. Half an hour later he and Hamad came over to us with a young man who greeted us and then told us to unload our camels and make ourselves comfortable; he said that when he had finished watering he would take us to his encampment. The caravan from Ibri watered their animals. One of them unexpectedly gave Hamad a small package of dates; they were very large and very sweet, but I was sick of dates and never wanted to see another. They moved off up the wadi and we then went over to the well, which had clean water at a depth of twenty feet.

In the afternoon the young herdsman, whose name was Ali, led us to his encampment two miles away. He agreed to take some of my party to Ibri, although we had been disconcerted to hear of the trouble there a few days earlier between the townsfolk and a party of Rashid. Ali asked me if I was going to Ibri, but I said that I was suffering from fever and would remain here to rest. Al Auf had told him already that I was from Syria, that I had recently been at Riyadh, and that I was now on my way to Salala. We agreed that bin Kabina and Musallim should remain with me while the others went to Ibri. Ali promised that when he returned from Ibri he would come with us to the Wadi al Amairi, where he could find us another *rabia* to take us through the rest of the Duru country. The party going to Ibri left in the morning; Ali said that they would be back in five days' time.

They were pleasant, lazy days. Staiyun, Ali's father, fed us on bread, dates, and milk and spent most of his time with us. The more I saw of the old man the more I liked him. I asked him about Umm al Samim, and he told me that the three wadis, al Ain, al Aswad, and al Amairi, ended in these quicksands about fifty miles to the west of us. He confirmed the stories I had already heard that raiding parties had been swallowed up in them, and said that he himself had seen a flock of goats disappear beneath the surface. I determined that I would come back and visit Umm al Samim and that I would try to penetrate into the mountains which were ruled by the Imam. It was interesting to collect from old Staiyun the information I should require to enable me to do this journey: about the tribes and their alliances, the different sheikhs and their rivalries, the Imam's government, and about wells and the distances that lay between them. But for the present I should be satisfied if I arrived at Bai without mishap and without delay; already I was worried, for five days and then six had passed and still there was no news of my companions.

Finally, my companions returned from Ibri. Hamad and Bakhit went back to their homes, and after Staiyun had fetched his nephew Muhammad the rest of us camped on the far side of the wadi. It took us eight hours to reach the Wadi al Aswad and two more long days to reach the Amairi. It was difficult to get the observations which I required for my mapping, and impossible to take photographs while Muhammad was with us. He enquired from the others why I did not pray, and they said that Syrians were evidently lax about their religion. We reached the well at Haushi near the southern coast six days after leaving the Amairi. We spent the next day there drying the meat, and then set off westwards for Bai, which we reached five days later. Seeing camels in the distance, Mabkhaut said, 'That is bin Turkia's camel and there is bin Anauf's.' We approached a ridge and suddenly a small figure showed up upon it. It was bin Anauf. 'They come! They come!' he screamed, and raced down the slope. Old Tamtaim appeared, hobbling towards us. I slid stiffly from my camel and greeted them. The old man flung his arms about me, with tears running down his face, too moved to be coherent. Bitter had been his wrath when the Bait Kathir returned from Ramlat al Ghafia. He said they had brought black shame upon his tribe by deserting me. It was 31 January. I had parted from them at Mughshin on 24 November. It seemed like two years.

Only Tamtaim, bin Turkia, and his son were here. The others were near the coast, where there was better grazing. Bin Turkia said he would take the news to them next day. We slept little that night. We talked and talked, and brewed coffee and yet more coffee, while we told them of our doings. They were Bedu, and no mere outline would suffice either them or my companions; what they wanted was a detailed account of all that we had seen and done, the people we had spoken to, what we had eaten and when and where. My companions seemed to have forgotten nothing. It was long past midnight when I lay down to sleep and they were still talking. Next day the others arrived with many Harasis who had come to see the Christian. Some women also turned up. There was much coming and going and much talk; only Sultan sat apart and brooded. My anxieties and difficulties were now over, but we still had far to go before we reached Salala.

We rode across the flatness of the Jaddat al Harasis, long marches of eight and even ten hours a day. We were like a small army, for many Harasis and Mahra travelled with us, going to Salala to visit the Sultan of Muscat, who had recently arrived there. I delighted in the surging rhythm of this mass of camels, the slapping shuffle of their feet, the shouted talk, and the songs which stirred the blood of men and beasts so that they drove forward with quickened pace. And there was life here. Gazelle grazed among the flat-topped acacia bushes, and once I saw a distant herd of oryx looking very white against the dark gravel

At Yisbub the water was fresh and maidenhair fern grew in the damp rock above the pool.

At Andhur, overlooking the Qarra forest.

of the plain. There were lizards, about eighteen inches in length, which scuttled across the ground.

We watered at Khaur Wir: I wondered how much more foul water could taste and still be considered drinkable. We watered again six days later at Yisbub. We went on again and reached Andhur, where I had been the previous year. Then we climbed up on to the Qarra mountains and looked upon the sea. It was nineteen days since we had left Bai. We descended the mountain in the afternoon and camped under great fig-trees beside the pools of Darbat. There were mallard and pintail and widgeon and coots on these pools, and that night Musallim shot a striped hyena. It was one of three which ran chuckling round our camp in the moonlight.

We had sent word into Salala, and next morning the Wali rode out to meet us accompanied by a crowd of townsfolk and Bedu. There were many Rashid with him, some of them old friends, others I had not yet met, among these bin Kalut who had accompanied Bertram Thomas. With him were the Rashid we had left at Mughshin, who told us that Mahsin had recovered and was in Salala.

The Wali feasted us in a tent beside the sea, and in the afternoon we went to the R.A.F. camp. My companions insisted on a triumphal entry, so we rode into the camp firing off our rifles, while ahead of us some Bait Kathir danced and sang, brandishing their daggers.

All of the Harasi women were masked with visor-like pieces of stiff black cloth, and one of them was dressed in white, which was unusual.

From Salala to Mukalla

A leisurely journey with the Rashid to Mukalla completes my survey of this part of Arabia.

I stayed at Salala for a week. I was busy writing up my notes, sorting out my collections, and arranging to travel with the Rashid to Mukalla.

I had come to Dhaufar determined to cross the Empty Quarter. I had succeeded and for me the venture needed no justification. I realized, however, that from the point of view of the Locust Research Centre my return journey through Oman was far more important than my crossing of the Sands. To them the only justification for this crossing would be that it had enabled me to enter Oman. From there I had brought back the information which the Locust Research Centre required. Dr Uvarov had thought that the river-beds which drained the western slopes of the ten-thousand-foot Jabal al Akhadar might carry down sufficient water to the Sands to produce permanent vegetation there, and that in consequence the mouths of the great wadis might be outbreak centres for the desert locusts. I had found out that floods were rare in the lower reaches of the wadis, and that when they occurred they dispersed in the sterile salt-flats of the Umm al Samim, where nothing grows.

I enjoyed the days I spent at Salala. It was a pleasant change talking English instead of the constant effort of talking Arabic; to have a hot bath and to eat well-cooked food; even to sit at ease on a chair with my legs stretched out, instead of sitting on the ground with them tucked under me. But the pleasure of doing these things was enormously enhanced for me by the knowledge that I was going back into the desert; that this was only an interlude and not the end of my journey.

I now planned to travel to Mukalla in the Eastern Aden Protectorate and to map the country along the watershed between the wadis which ran northwards to the Sands and those which ran southwards to the sea. A map of this area, together with the one which I had made the year before during my journey to the Hadhramaut, would establish the outline of the unknown country to the west of Dhaufar.

I arranged with bin Kalut that he and a party of Rashid should go with me to Mukalla. We agreed that I should pay for

Bin Kalut's son Muhammad (left, with myself and Sultan) was half-brother, through his mother, to Salim bin Kabina – a young man, heavily built like his father, amiable but rather ineffective.

Musallim bin al Kamam was a lean middle-aged man with a quick receptive mind and a relentless spirit which drove him so that he was the most widely travelled of the Rashid, and the most intelligent. I found him an amusing companion, quick to tell me anything that he thought might interest me.

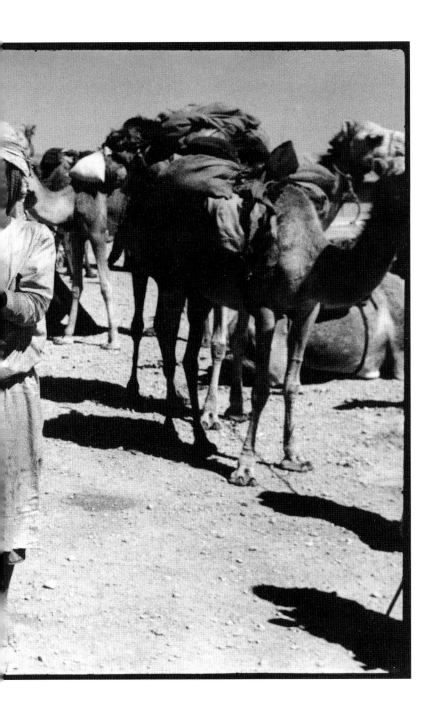

fifteen men, as I had done the previous year, but that the Rashid should settle among themselves how many actually accompanied me. A large force of Dahm had raided the Rashid and Manahil two months before, capturing many camels. Unfortunately bin Kalut could not travel with me now. A year before, he had concluded a two-year truce with the Dahm which this last raid had violated. Now he was going to demand the return of the Rashid camels that had been lifted. He undertook to find the necessary *rabias* from the tribes whose territory we should pass. I meanwhile paid off the Bait Kathir, except for Mabkhaut, bin Turkia, and his son bin Anauf. Musallim could not come with us because we should be travelling through Mahra country and, having killed one of them, he had a blood-feud with that tribe. Al Auf, bin Kabina, and the three Bait Kathir were to come, in addition to the party which bin Kalut was collecting.

On 3 March bin Kalut and about sixty Rashid turned up in the R.A.F. camp. A large number of Bait Kathir and other tribesmen camped with us that night at Al Ain. Musallim was among them, having come to see us off. Rather apprehensively, I asked bin Kalut how many of these people were going with us to Mukalla. He reassured me by saying that there would be only thirty Rashid, as well as my own party and *rabias* from the Bait Khawar, Mahra, and Manahil.

Next day we crossed the Kismim pass and camped once more by the pool of Aiyun. Bin Kabina was accompanied by a boy I had noticed the night before. They were about the same age. This boy was dressed only in a length of blue cloth wrapped round his waist with one tasselled end thrown over his right shoulder, and his dark hair fell like a mane about his shoulders. He told me that his name was Salim bin Ghabaisha and he asked me to take him with us. Bin Kabina urged me to let him join us, saying that he was the best shot in the tribe and as good a hunter as Musallim, so that if he was with us we should feed every day on meat, for there were many ibex and gazelle in the country ahead of us. He added, 'He is my friend. Let him come with us for my sake. The two of us will go with you wherever you want. We will always be your men.' I told bin Ghabaisha that he could come, and later when we camped I gave him one of my spare rifles to use until we reached Mukalla. Next morning he went off at dawn to hunt for ibex and he came back in the evening carrying across his shoulders a large ram which he had shot. I met few good hunters among the Bedu — only an occasional one of them possessed the necessary enthusiasm — but bin Ghabaisha was one of these, and Musallim bin Tafl was another.

After dinner bin Kabina got up from beside me, saying that he was going to fetch his camel. Suddenly someone called out, 'Bin Kabina has fallen down.' I looked round and saw him lying on the sand. He was unconscious when I reached him. His pulse was very feeble and his body cold; he was breathing hoarsely. I carried him to the fire and piled blankets on him to warm him. I then tried to pour a little brandy down his throat but he could not swallow. Gradually his breathing became easier and his body a little warmer, but he did not recover consciousness. The others crowded round and discussed the chances of his dying, until I could scarcely bear it; and then someone asked where we were going tomorrow and I said that there would be no tomorrow if bin Kabina died. Hours later as I lay beside him I felt him relax and knew that he was sleeping and was no longer unconscious. He woke at dawn and at first could hear but could not speak, and signed to me that his chest was hurting. By midday he could speak and in the evening he was all right again. The Rashid gathered round him, changing incantations and firing off their rifles; and then sprinkled flour, coffee, and sugar in the stream-bed to appease the spirits which they had exorcized. Later they slaughtered a goat, sprinkled him with its blood, and declared him cured. I have often wondered what was wrong with him and can only think it was some kind of fit.

Bin Ghabaisha had a face of classic beauty, pensive and rather sad in repose, but which lit up when he smiled, like a pool touched by the sun. Antinous must have looked like this, I thought, when Hadrian first saw him in the Phrygian woods. The boy moved with effortless grace, walking as women walk who have carried vessels on their heads since childhood. A stranger might have thought that his smooth, pliant body would never bear the rigours of desert life, but I knew how deceptively enduring were these Bedu boys who looked like girls.

I sat beside bin Kabina hour after hour wondering miserably if he was going to die. I remembered how I had first met him in the Wadi Mitan, how he had come to Shisur to join me, how he had unhesitatingly remained with me at Ramlat al Ghafa when the Bait Kathir had deserted me. I remembered his happiness when I gave him his rifle, and I knew that whenever I thought of the past months I should be thinking of him, for he had shared everything with me, even my doubts and difficulties. I remembered with bitter regret how I had sometimes vented my ill-temper on him to ease the strain under which I lived, and how he had always been good-tempered and very patient.

Almost daily bin Ghabaisha shot ibex or gazelle, and then bin Kabina cooked the meals of which he and I had dreamt when we had starved together in the Sands.

We travelled slowly, for I was in no hurry to reach Mukalla. After the slogging effort of the past months it was sheer enjoyment to dawdle along, on the watch, almost from the moment when we started, for somewhere to stop again. We would choose a spot in the cool shadow of a cliff, or else under some trees, where the tracery of branches threw a net of shade across the sand. There we would remain for the rest of the day or move on again in the evening, as the fancy took us. We had plenty of food and water, and there was acacia to feed our camels.

We remained for three days at Habarut. There was a constant passage of visitors to our camping place while we were there. A woman came over to us and I recognized her as Nura, whom I had met the year before. Her three small children were with her; only the eldest one, aged about nine, wore any clothes. She told me that they were camped four miles away, and that the children had insisted on coming to see me again when they heard I was here. I gave the children dates and sugar to eat, while I talked to Nura. She was unveiled, and like most of the women in this part of Arabia was dressed in dark blue. She had a strong, square, weather-beaten face, and wore a silver ring through her right nostril. I thought she was surprisingly old to have three small children. She talked in a rather husky voice, telling me how she was going down to Ghaidat al Mahra on the coast to get a load of sardines. As bin Ghabaisha had shot an ibex we had meat and soup for lunch. The children fed with us, but Nura was given a dish by herself. Arabs will not feed with women. Later, however, she returned and, sitting a little back from the circle, was given coffee and tea which she drank with the rest of us.

In the evening someone mentioned Nura. I asked if her husband was dead, and al Auf said, 'She has no husband. The children are bastards.' When I expressed my surprise he said that bin Alia, who was one of our party, was also 'a son of unlawfulness'. I asked if there was any slur attached to being a bastard, and bin Kabina said, 'No. It is not the child's fault,' and added jokingly, 'Next time, Umbarak, you see a girl that pleases you, sit down next to her in the dark, push your camel-stick through the sand until it is underneath her, and then turn it over until the crook presses against her. If she gets up, gives you an indignant look, and marches off, you will know that you are wasting your time. If she stays where she is, you can meet her next day when she is herding the goats.' I said, 'If it is as easy as all that there must be plenty of bastards,' and someone answered, 'Not among the Rashid, but the Humum near Mukalla have a whole section composed entirely of bastards.'

These families of Mahra were watering their camels at the shallow wells of Habarut beside the tangled palm groves.

The general belief among the English people that Arab women are kept shut up is true of many of the women in the towns, but not among the tribes. Not only is it impossible for a man to shut up his wife when he is living under a tree, or in a tent which is always open on one side, but he requires her to work, to fetch water and firewood, and to herd the goats. If a woman thinks she is being neglected or ill-treated by her husband she can easily run away to her father or brother. Her husband has then to follow her and try to persuade her to come back. Her family will certainly take her part, insisting that she has been monstrously ill-treated. In the end the husband will probably have to give her a present before he can induce her to return. Wives cannot divorce their husbands, but the husband may agree to divorce his wife if she has refused to live with him, on condition that he recovers the two or three camels which he gave as the bride-price. If, however, he divorces her of his own accord he does not get these camels back.

From Habarut we climbed up on to the Daru plateau, a featureless gravel plain which drains to the sea. We came across some crude shelters with walls of rock and roofs of branches overlaid with earth and supported on pillars of piled stones. But they were all empty, since seven rainless years had driven the Bait Khawar down into the valley of the Kidyut, which starts here as a deep sheer-sided canyon. I climbed down into this with some of my companions, while the others took the camels round by an easier route. A small spring trickled out from among the limestone slabs which had fallen from the precipices above. Some Mahra were watering camels and filling goatskins. One of their women had stained her face green, and another had blue and green stripes painted down her nose and chin, and across her cheeks. The effect was not only weird but repulsive. I was on the point of suggesting to bin Kabina that both of them would be more alluring if they were veiled, when a small boy about ten years old darted over to us. He was Said, bin Kabina's brother. He was trying desperately to be dignified, but could not hide his excitement. He assured me at once that he was coming with us, and pointed to the camel which I had given to bin Kabina the year before, saying, 'There is my mount.' I asked him where his rifle was and he waved his stick and said that this would have to do unless I gave him one. Suddenly we heard many voices shouting on the cliff above us. A party of Bait Khawar were refusing passage to our camels, saying that the Christian might not pass through their valley. A scuffle had started, and it looked as if there might be a fight, until our *rabia* drove his tribesmen back, and the camels came lurching down the steep path to join us in the valley-bottom. Said said scornfully, 'They are only Bait Khawar,' and went on to tell me how he had heard that we should pass this way and had ridden for two days to meet us.

A large, vociferous, but badly-armed crowd of Bait Khawar had collected and they insisted that I could not pass down the valley unless I paid them money. I refused, saying that I had a *rabia* and was entitled to pass, but they went on shouting that I must give them money if I wished to see their valley. I knew that there would be no end to our troubles if I once paid blackmail. I have never done so and had no intention of doing so now. In the Western Aden Protectorate European travellers are constantly held up, since the tribes have learnt that they can extort money from them. Our *rabia*, an old man with tired faded eyes and a straggling white beard, said furiously that he would take me through the valley if I wished to go in defiance of his whole tribe, since they had no right to stop us. However, the gathering broke up without reaching an agreement. Many of the Bait Khawar who had been defying us a few minutes earlier came over to our camping place to chat with us and give us their news.

That evening we discussed what we should do. The general opinion was that the Bait Khawar were bluffing, since they were defying tribal custom and had no reason for their behaviour except avarice, but bin Kalut, al Auf and others asked me how much it would matter if we followed the path along the top of the cliffs. This was the route we had indeed originally planned to take, but the Rashid had wished to travel down the valley, where they thought that there would be better grazing for their camels. Bin Kalut pointed out that if some fool did shoot at us and hit anyone it would start a war between tribes who were traditionally allied. I willingly agreed to take the top road, which indeed suited me better, since, for the purpose of mapping, I should overlook the valley and the country on both sides of it. In any case, the last thing I wished to do was to cause trouble among the tribes. I knew that my freedom of movement in the desert depended on my reputation for harming no one.

Said bin Kabina's brother (right, with Musallim bin Anauf) had large sparkling eyes, very white teeth, and a face as fresh as a half-opened flower. I asked him who would look after his mother and sister if he came with us to Mukalla, and he assured me that they were with his uncle and that they would be all right without him. I decided to let him come and he trotted happily off to tell bin Kabina.

We descended into the valley again where it joins the Mahrat to form the Jiza. There were palm groves and small settlements, with a little cultivation in all these valleys. The Jiza bends in a great arc, draining the greater part of the Mahra country, before it finally enters the sea near Ghaidat, the largest of the Mahra villages. All this country was completely unmapped, but I was now able to fix its general outlines. My companions wished to travel due west to the Masila, which is the name of the lower reaches of the Wadi al Hadhramaut, but the Gumsait Mahra refused to let us pass. They collected in our camp in the evening and explained that they were prepared to take me through their country, provided that I hired their camels and sent the Rashid who were with me back to their homes. The Mahra are Ghafaris, and are usually on terms of armed neutrality with the Rashid and Bait Kathir. Since we had no *rabia* from their section their attitude seemed to me reasonable, but I had no intention of parting with the Rashid.

We were held up again in the Mahrat, this time by the Amarjid, who had probably heard that we had been turned back by the Gumsait. They, too, offered to take me on provided I sent

Sulaim, our Mahra rabia, belonged to the Amarjid, and he said that he could frank us through the Mahra tribes along the upper Mahrat as far as the watershed, beyond which lay the country of the Manahil. This route suited me better than the other, since by following it I should be able to fix the watershed as far as the Masila.

Fifteen years earlier, watching the coronation of Haile Selassie as King of Kings of Ethiopia, I had been fascinated by the continuity, however tenuous, which linked that ceremony with Solomon and Sheba. Now watching these half-naked Mahra, with their indigo-smeared figures, sitting beneath the dying palms in the Wadi Jiza, discussing our movements in a language which had once been spoken by Minaeans, Sabaeans, and Himyarites, I realized that here was a link with the past even older and more authentic, for scholars believe that the Mahra are descended from the ancient Habasha, who colonized Ethiopia as long ago as the first millennium B.C. and gave their name to the Abyssinians. I myself had discovered the year before a mountain called Jabal Habashiya which was only fifty miles to the west of our present camp.

accompany us for two days. A little later one of them came back and said that, as they had no animals here with which to feast us, they would forgo the payment of these men. I then gave them an equivalent sum as a present and everyone was satisfied.

Three days later we crossed the watershed between the wadis flowing to the north and to the south, a flat rocky plateau about a quarter of a mile across. To the south the country was very broken and there were many deep gorges, while to the north a number of broad valleys, whose beds were of gravel and hard sand, started abruptly from the foot of the escarpment. I watched an eagle chasing a gazelle and a little later saw two ibex. These were very common both here and on the cliffs above the Mahrat.

We arrived at Dahal well three days later. The water, which stank of sulphur, was at the end of a tunnel through the limestone rock and was difficult to reach.

In the afternoon a small party of Manahil turned up with some goats. They warned us that two hundred and fifty Dahm were raiding the country ahead of us, and had killed seven

said that they themselves intended to seek refuge among the Mahra. Beyond Dahal the land was empty; everyone had fled, either across the watershed or down into the valley of the Masila, which it took us three more days to reach. The country was very broken, and the only possible route for our camels was along the bottom of deep canyons, which cut the limestone plateau into blocks. We pushed scouts out ahead when we were travelling, and posted sentries whenever we stopped, for we were well aware what would happen to us if we were trapped by the Dahm in the bottom of one of these sheer-sided gorges.

When we reached the shrine of Nabi Hud in the Masila, we found many Manahil collected there with their camels, sheep, and goats. They told us that one party of raiders, believed to be seventy strong, had surprised an encampment of six Manahil in the nearby Wadi Hun. One of them had escaped, but no one knew what happened to the others. They also said that another and much larger force was raiding in the steppes to the north. Eighty Manahil had gone off up the Wadi Hun in pursuit.

Wadi Jiza near its junction with the Mahrat.

We decided to move up the valley of the Masila to the village of Fughama, where we were told that bin Tanas, the Manahil Sheikh, was collecting his fighting men. Bin Duailan — the most famous raider in southern Arabia, who had joined my party in Salala — went on ahead to tell him that we were coming, and that we would join him in an attack upon the Dahm if he could find out where they were. I had been uncertain whether the Rashid would agree to this, since they were still nominally at peace with the Dahm, but they said at once that, acting under my orders, they would consider themselves to be *askar,* or soldiers, not bound by tribal custom.

We stayed there for another day, in case there was any more news of the raiders, and on 14 April we started for Mukalla, the journey's end that I had no desire to reach. Dawdling away the days, we mounted through narrow, twisting gorges, among piles of fallen rock, to the large village and palm groves of Ghail ba Yamin. We crossed the stony blackened table land, known to the Arabs as al Jaul, descended to the coast near Shihr, and arrived at Mukalla on 1 May.

Sheppard, who was the Resident in Mukalla, arranged for the Arabs who were with me to stay in the Beduin Legion camp on the outskirts of the town. I left them there and went down to the Residency to get a bath and to change into the clothes which had arrived from Salala. Later, having washed, shaved off my beard, and put on European clothes, I went back to the camp. My party was in a large building. As I approached, bin Anauf called out, 'There is a Christian coming'. Realizing that he had not recognized me, I went to the door and stood there looking uncertain. Bin Turkia spoke to me and I answered in English. Someone said, 'Bring him in'; another person told them to make coffee, and someone else asked, 'Do the Christians drink coffee?' They spread a rug for me and signed to me to sit down. Bin Kabina, bin Ghabaisha, al Auf, Mabhkaut, and old bin Kalut were all there looking at me. Suddenly bin Kabina said, 'By God, it is Umbarak!' and seized me by the shoulders with playful violence. I had not realized I looked so different. I said, 'How would you like me to travel with you dressed like this?' and they said, 'No one would go with you like that. You look like a Christian.'

On his last evening in Mukalla, bin Kabina showed me what he had bought — a load of grain, two pounds of coffee-beans, two cooking-pots, three water-skins, a length of rope, a ball of string, two packing needles, a dozen boxes of matches, four yards of dark blue cloth for his mother, a loin-cloth for himself, and a penknife. When I suggested he should have bought some blankets, he said, 'Camels are what I want. I can buy three more with the money which you have given me. With Qamaiqam, and the camel I bought in Salalah, and the one you gave me last year I shall have six. Now I am rich. I am used to hardship. Cold won't hurt me. I am a Bedu.'

Mukalla, which we reached on 1 May.

The village of Ghail ba Yamin.

Preparations for a Second Crossing

> *I return to Arabia with the intention of crossing the Western Sands. From the Hadhramaut I journey through the country of the Saar and with my Rashid companions, make ready at Manwakh well.*

From Mukalla I went to the Hajaz, and travelled there for three months, going as far as Najran in the country of the Yam, on the north-western edge of the Empty Quarter. Then I returned to London.

In deserts, however arid, I have never felt homesick for green fields and woods in spring, but now that I was in England I longed with an ache that was almost physical to be back in Arabia. The Locust Control Centre offered me a new job supervising the destruction of locusts in the Hajaz, with a good salary, all expenses paid, and the prospect of permanent employment. But it was not enough. I wanted the wide emptiness of the Sands, the fascination of unknown country, and the company of the Rashid.

The Western Sands offered the challenge which I required in order to find a purpose for another journey. To cross them would be to complete the exploration of the Empty Quarter. Two years earlier I had thought of doing this journey. King Ibn Saud had however emphatically refused permission when our Ambassador had asked for it — and, in any case, it had been too late in the season to go there when I reached the Hadhramaut from Dhaufar. Now I made up my mind to make this crossing. I should be defying the King, but I hoped that I should be able to water at some well on the far side of the Sands and then slip away unobserved. I was certain that some of the Rashid would accompany me, and with them I should have the freedom of the desert. I therefore wired to Sheppard at Mukalla asking him to send a messenger to bin Kabina at Habarut telling him, bin al Kamam, and bin Ghabaisha to meet me in the Hadhramaut at the time of the new moon in November. If I kept the party small I could pay for the journey with the money I had saved. The future could take care of itself.

I arrived in Mukalla on 3 November and, after staying for a few days with Sheppard and collecting the rifles and ammunition which I had left with him the year before, I went up to Saiwun where I stayed with Watts, the Political Officer. Watts was having trouble with the Manahil. Some of them had

Buildings such as these were scattered everywhere in Yam country and one would just happen upon them.

A scene in Yam country where the culture of the land has made the people sedentary, as opposed to the Bedu.

recently surprised two government posts in the Hadhramaut and captured a large number of rifles and much ammunition. One Bedu legionary had been killed. Since the Manahil refused to hand back the rifles, Watts had forbidden any of them to come into the towns.

We visited the well at Manwakh, in the Aiwat al Saar which drains to the Sands and of which the Raidat is a tributary. I was glad to have a look at this well, knowing that I must start my journey across the Empty Quarter either from it or from Zamakh. We found some Saar watering camels and goats. The water was fresh and I noticed that they mixed rock-salt in it before watering their camels.

As there was no news of bin Kabina and the others, I decided to travel for a fortnight in the Saar country before I started on my journey across the Sands, in order to link up the traverses which I had made in southern Arabia, between the Halfain and the Hadhramaut, with Philby's work in 1936 along the Yemen border. The Saar, a large and powerful tribe, have been aptly described as 'the wolves of the desert'. They were hated and feared by all the south Arabian desert tribes, whom they harried unmercifully, raiding as far eastward as Mughshin and the Jaddat al Harasis, and northwards to the Yam, the Dawasir, and the Murra. Boscawen had hunted oryx in their country in 1931, and Ingrams paid a cursory visit to the edge of their territory in 1934; otherwise no Englishman had been there.

Watts found in Shibam two Saar who said they would take me into their country. One of them, called Salim, was a lively little man in a blue loin-cloth. The other was tall and was called Ahmad.

We went up to Raidat al Saar. Ahmad told me the inhabitants had died in the great famine in 1943. The terraced valley was green with crops of sorghum and beans, planted on floods in July; and there were clumps of date palms and many *ilb* trees. Raidat is the heart of the Saar country, but lacks permanent water. The inhabitants had recently tried to dig a well but had abandoned it when they failed to find water at sixty feet. In the Saar country there are only two permanent wells, one at Manwakh about 180 feet, and the other at Zamakh, which they told me was 240 feet deep.

The Saar, many of whom were collected in the Raidat to harvest the crops, had heard of me as a result of my wanderings in southern Arabia and welcomed me with great friendliness. I found them a pleasant, virile people, without the corroding avarice of the Bait Kathir. Other tribes call them treacherous, but this is probably a slander inspired by dislike. However, their reputation for godlessness is well merited in Arab eyes, since they neither fast nor pray, saying that the Prophet Muhammad gave their forefathers a dispensation from both.

Raidat al Saar is a shallow valley about two hundred yards across, running through a barren limestone plateau. On the low cliffs which enclosed it were stone buildings and watch-towers, many of them empty.

Like all the southern Bedu, the Saar are a small, lightly-built race. A few wore rags round their heads but most of them were bareheaded.

The Saar told me some Rashid were camped near by. We went over to them next day and found one-eyed Abdullah, Muhammad, who was bin Kalut's son, and some Awamir and Mahra sheikhs. When I was close they fired shots low over my head, their usual greeting for sheikhs or other distinguished people. About forty Saar were with them, discussing the renewal of a truce with the Rashid. Muhammad told me that bin Kabina had received my letter at Habarut and that he had ridden down to Ghaidat on the coast to find someone to translate it. I knew that it was at least a hundred miles from Habarut to Ghaidat and realized this extra distance would account for his not having arrived yet. However, it was good to know that he was on the way. Muhammad also told me that bin al Kamam was still in the Yemen, negotiating with the Dahm for the return of the Rashid camels, and that bin Ghabaisha was in Dhaufar. Taking me aside he asked where I was going and I told him, but begged him to keep it secret since I knew that it would be dangerous if the tribes

learnt of my movements in advance. He volunteered to come with me and I accepted his offer, as it seemed unlikely that I should be able to get hold of either bin al Kamam or bin Ghabaisha. We agreed to meet in the Raidat at the time of the next new moon. He could not come with me now, as the discussions with the Saar would go on for some days.

The news here was all of raids and rumours of raids. The desert was more disturbed than it had been for years. Muhammad pressed me to spend the night with them, but I was anxious to get back to the Hadhramaut now that I knew that bin Kabina had received my message. Two days later we were near Tamis well, which belongs to the Awamir. This was dangerous border country. Ahmad went on ahead to scout as we approached the well. A little later he came back and signalled to us to be quiet and to stay where we were. When he got up to us he told us that a large party of Manahil were coming up the main valley. I went with him to look. He warned me to keep well out of

There was a very lovely girl working with the others on the well. Her hair was braided, except where it was cut in a fringe across her forehead, and fell in a curtain of small plaits round her neck. She wore various silver ornaments and several necklaces, some of large cornelians, others of small white beads. Round her waist she had half a dozen silver chains, and above them her sleeveless blue tunic gaped open to show small firm breasts. She was very fair. When she saw I was trying to take a photograph of her she screwed up her face and stuck out her tongue at me. Salim, thinking to help me, had told her not to move and explained what I was doing. During the following days both he and Ahmad chaffed me whenever I was silent, saying that I was thinking of the girl at Manwakh, which was frequently true.

sight, since he said the Manahil hated the Saar, and that after their attacks on the government posts in the Hadhramaut they might well feel that they were at war with the Christians. He added that, anyway, they were raiders who had suffered losses and would be in a savage mood. Peering cautiously between some rocks I saw about twenty men just disappearing round a corner a quarter of a mile away. They were driving some camels with them and were riding in silence with their rifles in their hands. They were naked except for their dark-blue loin-cloths. If they had been ten minutes later they would have found us on the well. We remained where we were till late in the afternoon, and then after Ahmad had looked to see that there was no-one about, we went up to fill our water-skins. There were fresh tracks everywhere. Ali said he had seen about forty mounted men with about thirty captured camels, and explained that the main party would have split up into several groups after the raid in order to make pursuit more difficult.

There was excellent water at fifteen feet in a hole in the rock. A loopholed *sangar* overlooked it from the cliff immediately above. Although it was getting late we went on again after filling our water-skins, so as not to camp near the well, always a dangerous thing to do in disturbed country. We found a shallow cave and stopped there, since the weather was cloudy and looked like rain. After dinner, as we were making tea and chatting quietly, a voice suddenly said 'Salam alaikum'. We grabbed our rifles, which were beside us, unable owing to the firelight to see into the darkness. I answered, and Amair dropped off his camel and came forward to greet us. He told me that he had come with bin Kabina from Habarut and that bin Kabina had foundered his camel and had stopped with Muhammad to await my return.

The Saar raised the water by hand, the long ropes of palmetto fibre running over pulleys attached to a wooden scaffolding round the well. The southern Bedu do not use camels to draw the well-ropes, as is done on the deep wells in the Najd, although villagers in the Hadhramaut use camels and oxen to raise the trip-buckets from which they water their cultivations. After the Saar had finished watering they took their ropes, pulleys, and leather watering-troughs away with them.

Salim bin Ghabaisha.

I asked Amair for news of bin Ghabaisha and he said that he was with his father at Mudhail. Later I asked him if he thought that bin Ghabaisha would fly to Mukalla from Salala if I could arrange it, but he said, 'No, he is only a boy. If you were with him he might go in an aeroplane but he won't go by himself with the Christians.'

Thirteen days after leaving Shibam, we camped once more on the plateau above the Hadhramaut. We have travelled 225 miles. For the last three days the sky had been overcast, and that night we saw continuous flickers of lightning far away to the north. Amair watched with intent eyes, and several times exclaimed, 'God willing, we will have a year of plenty.'

Next morning we scrambled down the high cliffs into the Hadhramaut itself. Below us we could see the Sultan's palace at Saiwun, massive and very white above the dark wall of palms. Other buildings, too, with crenellated towers, and minarets, and glistening domes, stood among green fields and gardens filled with fruit-trees.

I always felt imprisoned in the Hadhramaut; I should have been interested to see it ten years earlier, before Ingrams had established law and order; for it was very old, a fragment from a vanished world that had survived in this remote valley. But now the spoiling hand of progress was on the land.

Walking through Saiwun, the largest town in the Hadhramaut with about twenty thousand inhabitants, I felt that it would not be long before there were cinemas, and wirelesses blaring at street corners. Watts was on leave in Aden but

I stayed with Johnson, his assistant. Despite Amair's scepticism, I sent a telegram to the Air Officer Commanding at Aden. I asked whether the C.O. at Salala could get hold of bin Ghabaisha through the Wali, and if he was successful — whether bin Ghabaisha could be flown to Riyan and then sent up to Saiwun by car. A week later I got a reply: 'Bin Ghabaisha contacted Stop Leaving by air for Riyan tomorrow.'

Two days later Johnson was entertaining the Saiwun and Tarim football teams to tea in his house. I was busy handing cakes to the Tarim centre-forward when I heard a well-known voice saying 'Salam alaikum' and in walked bin Ghabaisha. He was wearing his dagger and carried a camel stick. He had nothing else with him. He sat down beside me, and I asked him where he had come from.

'We were near Mudhail, in the wadi where you stopped on your way to Mukalla,' he said. 'I and my brother were herding our camels when one of the Wali's slaves arrived. The slave said that you had arrived, and that the Wali had sent for me; so I told my brother to take the camels back in the evening and to tell my father I had gone to Salala. When I got there I went in to see the Wali in the palace he said to me, "Umbarak is in the Hadhramaut and has sent for you; an aeroplane is going there tomorrow. Will you go there in it?" '

I interrupted to ask what his answer had been.

He replied: 'I said, "Why would I not go in an aeroplane? The Wali then sent me to the Christians' camp. The Christians gave me food — horrid stuff; I did not like it, I slept there and next afternoon the aeroplane arrived.'

I asked: 'Had you ever seen an aeroplane before?' and he answered, 'Yes, on my way back from Mukalla last year; it was very high up but it made more noise than this one. When I got into the aeroplane the Christians tried to tie me with a rope. I would not let them.'

I asked him how he had liked flying.

He said: 'It was all right when we flew over the ground. I could see the wadis and hills — I knew where I was. By God, Umbarak, once I saw men and camels, very small like ants! I was frightened when we flew over the sea. When it got dark I thought the Christians had lost their way. They all began to chatter and wave their arms about. When we arrived at Riyan an Arab interpreter said that I was to go to Aden in the morning. The man was a fool, so I went to one of the Christians who had driven the aeroplane. I told him you were in the Hadhramaut. At first none of them could understand me, but at last they said "Aiwah! Aiwah! Umbarak — Hadhramaut," and hit me on the back and then gave me tea and bread. They had put milk in the tea and I would not drink it. This morning they mounted me on a lorry and now I am here.'

He asked me where I was going, and I told him that I planned to cross the Empty Quarter to the Wadi Dawasir and to go from there to the Trucial Coast. All he said was, 'I have not got a rifle,' so I took him into my room and told him to choose one of the five rifles there. When he had chosen one I told him it was a present.

A young boy in the courtyard of a Saiwun house.

We spent two days in Shibam, the most interesting of these towns. Here Amair and bin Ghabaisha arranged with the Saar for camels to take us to the Raidat and bought such things as we still required. I had brought flour, rice, sugar, tea, and coffee from Mukalla, and we now purchased dried shark-meat, butter, spices, saddle-bags, ropes, and water-skins. I bought the water-skins myself, and among them I was palmed off with several sheepskins which invariably sweat when filled with water. This would not have happened if Amair or bin Ghabaisha had been with me, but they were busy elsewhere.

We left Shibam on 17 December and went up to Raidat. Ali bin Sulaiman of the Hatim section of the Saar who was with us was to be extremely helpful. The land was filled with rumours and alarms. Abdullah bin Nura, usually known by his family name of bin Maiqal, had recently arrived at Manwakh with the bin Maaruf Saar. Although these bin Maaruf belong to the Hatim section of the Saar, they no longer lived upon the Saar plateau but in the sands and steppes to the north, and for a dozen years had acknowledged Ibn Saud as their overlord and paid him tribute through the Amir at Najran. They were grazing their herds in the desert south of Najran when word reached them that the Yam and Dawasir were massing, having been authorized by Ibn Saud to attack the Saar and other Hadhramaut tribes in retaliation for the recent raids in which some of them had been implicated. They therefore fled southward to seek refuge among their kinsmen.

The Saar had evacuated the country between Al Abr and Zamakh, and it seemed probable that they would also abandon Manwakh and withdraw into the broken country along the middle Makhia. It was important for me to reach this well before they deserted it if I was to find guides and camels for my journey across the Sands.

I left the Raidat at once and arrived at Manwakh late in the evening of 28 December. There was no one near the well. As we had had a long day we decided to camp near by. At sunset six bin Maaruf came past. They were all young men and rode magnificent camels. They were worried by some camel-tracks which they had found farther up the valley. These they had been unable to identify, and they feared they might be tracks of Yam scouts, for Bedu push scouts out far ahead to locate an encampment and then after an all-night march fall on it at dawn. They told us that bin Maiqal was two hours away, and advised us not to camp where we were. We did not wish to arrive at the Saar encampment in the dark, so we decided to move into a side valley and spent the night there. I sent Amair to tell Muhammad and bin Kabina that we had arrived. Having camped, I think we all wished we had gone on after all, for the low rocky bluffs and empty plain looked menacing in the dying light and made us feel very lonely.

Shibam is surrounded by a high wall, but this is dwarfed by the close-packed houses, which rise inside it to seven or eight storeys.

Built on the edge of the dry river-bed, on a low mound in the middle of the valley, Shibam had a population of about seven thousand.

We cooked a quick meal and then put out the fire; Ali advised us not to talk. In the night one of our camels suddenly got to its feet. I had been lightly asleep and in a second was awake. The others crouched about me, their rifles pointing into the darkness. Ali said, 'It is only the camel,' and seizing its head-rope jerked at it until the grumbling animal subsided once more upon its knees. We lay down again, tense after this alarm.

In the sharp cold of the winter morning we rode to the Saar camp, passing herds of fat milch camels, which the herdsboys had just driven out to pasture. I noticed with anxiety that several families had already struck their tents and loaded their camels. The small children were seated in camel-litters, the first I had seen in southern Arabia, though I was familiar with them in the north. I hoped these preparations did not mean that the Saar were leaving Manwakh. As we approached, the bin Maaruf formed up to receive us and greeted us by firing low over our heads, before sweeping down on us, yelling and brandishing their daggers. We got off our camels to greet their sheikhs and some Karab, Manahil, and Mahra who were with them.

Bin Kabina had led the wild rush which welcomed us and I was glad indeed to see him. He looked well, but his shirt was in ribbons. There were, however, new clothes for him in my saddle-bags.

At first sight the bin Maaruf were very different from the other Saar. They wore long white shirts, cut with pointed sleeves which reached to the ground, and head-cloths and head-ropes of northern fashion.

We required nine camels, and next day my Rashid wandered round the encampments making inquiries. We knew that we should have to pay high prices, for we could get them nowhere else and we were in a hurry. We each of us needed a riding camel, as Muhammad, bin Kabina, and Amair had decided to leave theirs, which were in poor condition, with some Manahil who were here on a visit. I decided to buy four baggage camels since we should have a very long way to go before we reached the Trucial Coast. Bin Ghabaisha, who was a good judge, soon found himself a black *hazmia* for the equivalent of fifteen pounds. We chaffed him about his choice, for there is a prejudice against riding these black camels, but he said that she was a fine animal — which she was — and that he needed her for work and not for display. Whenever anyone approached her she flipped her tail up and down in a ridiculous manner, a sign that she had recently been served successfully.

Bin Kabina bought a young grey with a very long stride. She was six months gone in calf, but this would not matter since camels carry their young for a year. Gradually we collected the number we needed. I bought a small thoroughbred from Oman, a very willing animal but with an irritatingly short stride.

We needed a guide. Ali told me that bin Daisan, a middle-aged man from the bin Maaruf, knew these Western Sands better than anyone else. We spent several evenings in bin Daisan's tent trying to persuade him to come with us. I offered him money and a rifle, but avarice fought a losing battle in his mind with the caution that comes with middle age. Each night, by the time we left him, he would have agreed to come with us, but in the morning we would get a message saying that his family refused to agree.

Everyone assured us that we should certainly be killed by the Yam or the Dawasir as soon as we met them on the far side of the Sands. They told us that three large parties of Yam were even then raiding round Al Abr and had killed two Saar a few days ago. They said contemptuously that my Rashid were too young and inexperienced to know what lay ahead of us. Young they certainly were, for Muhammad was perhaps twenty-five years old, Amair twenty, and bin Kabina and bin Ghabaisha seventeen, yet they refused to be intimidated or to desert me. Muhammad suggested one evening that instead of crossing to the Wadi Dawasir we should cross the Sands farther to the east through Dakaka, but when I told him that Thomas and Philby had already been there and that it was the Western Sands that I wished to explore, he said, 'Don't worry. We will go with you wherever you want to go, whatever the Saar may say.' However, we agreed that we must get hold of a Saar to come with us so as to have protection from that tribe.

The small, black, goat-hair tents of the Saar were scattered about the valley.

Naked infants romped round the tents, and dark-clad women sat churning butter or moved about getting sticks or herding goats.

Many of the Saar, who hate the Rashid, were talking almost openly of following us when we left and killing us in the Sands. Not only were there bitter scores to settle between these two tribes, but they knew that I had a lot of money with me, as well as our rifles, ammunition, and camels. Our Manahil friends warned us against going without a Saar *rabia,* and yet where were we to get one? Two young Karab had volunteered to come with us, but they neither knew these sands nor would their presence protect us from the Saar.

Ali and I went back again to bin Daisan, and at last, after I had offered him more money, he agreed to accompany us.

We arranged to water our camels and fill our water-skins next day and to leave the day after that. Next morning as we were getting ready, a Mahra arrived from Shagham well, in the nearby Makhia, with news of bin Murzuk and the Abida raiders. They had looted the Rashid and Manahil and captured many camels and killed two Rashid herdsmen. The Mahra told us that the Abida had themselves been surprised while watering in the dark on Thamud well, and that five of them had been killed, but that the pursuit party, which was small, had been driven off. He had seen and spoken with the Abida at Shagham two days before; they had two very badly wounded men with them, and were consequently moving slowly on their way back to their own country, angry at their losses. He advised us to wait for a few days before we started. Though I was almost superstitiously unwilling to put off our departure, now that bin Daisan had at last made up his mind to go with us, I realized that there was nothing else to do. Everyone assured me that the raiders under bin Murzuk would follow us and kill us without mercy, if they, or any other Abida who were behind them, crossed our tracks.

The pursuit party had used as their battle-cry *Murzuk ya talabta* (Death to Murzuk), a battle-cry obviously invented for the occasion, and this for some reason convinced the Rashid that the pursuers had been from their own tribe, and neither Manahil nor Mahra. They were desperately anxious for every scrap of information about the raid, and especially about one of the pursuers who had been killed in the fight at Thamud. The Mahra repeated to them the description of this man, as he had heard it from the Abida, and he also described his rifle which he had seen. Muhammad and the others said, 'It is Salim bin Mautlauq; without a doubt it is Salim,' but they were puzzled by the description of the rifle, which they said belonged to no-one in their tribe. For weeks they were to discuss this question, hoping against hope that it was not Salim bin Mautlauq who had been killed. We did not hear what had happened until a year later on the Trucial Coast.

About twenty-five Rashid and a few Mahra had followed the Abida and found them watering their camels at Thamud. They knew that water was short and that, as the Abida numbered about a hundred and fifty, they would be all night watering their animals. They had crept towards the well. It was a cloudy night and they had got close before they were challenged. They fired a volley and then rushed the Abida using their daggers. Hopelessly outnumbered, they were soon driven back. When they collected again, where they had left their camels, they found that Salim was missing. A Mahra said that he had been killed near the well and produced his rifle. He explained that he had picked it up,

leaving his own rifle which was no good. Saud, Salim's brother, said at once that he was going back and the others went with him. When they reached the well there was no-one there and no sign of Salim. At dawn they followed the tracks which he had made as he had crawled away. They found him a mile away, unconscious, shot through the chest and neck. When he recovered consciousness he told them that a fatally wounded Abida had called out, 'Is there not one of them dead that I may look on him before I die?' and that someone had then seized him by the legs and dragged him over to the dying man, round whom many people were collected, the dying man had cursed him, and then someone had shot him again. When he came to, there was no one there and he had crawled off into the dark trying to get to the place where the Rashid had left their camels. He recovered from his wounds a few months afterwards.

Two days later we went to the well at Manwakh. We travelled there with a family that was camped near us. They said we could

Manwakh was one of the only two wells which were regarded as having permanent water in the Saar country, an area larger than Yorkshire. Yet now it had run dry after watering a couple of hundred camels, even though there had been a good rain six months earlier in the year. I wondered how the Saar managed for water in the summer and in years of drought.

use their gear for watering. The man rode a camel loaded with great coils of rope, with pulleys, well-buckets, rolled up water-skins, and a large watering-trough fashioned from skins stretched over a framework of wooden hoops. His son rode bareback on one of seven camels, and a woman and two small children drove a herd of goats. Others, too, were going down to the water. It was six miles away and we took two hours to get there. When we arrived there was already a crowd round the well mouth. Men and women drew on the ropes together, singing as they pulled, hand over hand. On each rope, as one bucket jerked up from the dark depths, slopping water down the glistening walls, another descended empty. Rows of bulging black skins lay upon the sand, guarded from the trampling feet of men and beasts by shrill-voiced children. Camels were watered, couched, and later driven away; men shouted with harsh voices to watchful, darting herdsboys; goats bleated, camels roared, the singing at the well-head rose and fell, the sun climbed higher, and the dark stain of spilt water spread farther across the ground.

Abdullah bin Nura and several elders arrived. They told us that they would not allow bin Daisan or anyone else from the bin Maaruf to go with us, and advised us to give up our plan to cross the Sands, as the Yam would certainly kill us if we did. I had half expected bin Daisan to let me down. We answered little and went

apart to talk it over. Ali suggested that two young Saar from his own section of the Hatim might go with us if I gave each of them a rifle and fifty cartridges. They had never crossed the Sands but had watered at the Hassi near Sulaiyil and were confident that they could find the well once we had arrived on the other side. He said that if they were with us we should be safe from the Saar. I asked the Rashid what they thought, and Muhammad answered, 'We are your men. We will go where you go. It is for you to decide.' I told bin Kabina to make coffee while I thought it over, and we went and sat beneath the cliff, where we had unloaded our camels. It seemed crazy to try to cross the Empty Quarter without a guide. It was about four hundred waterless miles, which would take at least sixteen days, and bin Daisan had told me that the dunes were very high and difficult. I remembered how hard had been the journey which we had done the year before, and how little margin we had to spare, even when guided by al Auf. I asked the Rashid if they thought we could get across without a guide, and Muhammad said, 'We live in the Sands. We can take you across without a guide. The danger will be from the Yam after we have got to the other side.' I told Ali that we would go, and asked him to fetch the two Saar, and he said he would bring them in the evening.

Unlike my companions, I was far more concerned with the physical difficulties of crossing the Empty Quarter, especially without a guide, than worried by what would happen to us if we ran into Arabs on the far side. I did not think that they would take us for raiders, since we would be leading four laden camels. I knew that our clothes and saddling would show them that we came from the south and belonged to the hated Mishqas, but I hoped to be able to get speech with any Arabs we might meet before they opened fire; and if they belonged to Ibn Saud I thought they might hesitate to kill us once they discovered I was a European, for fear of the King's anger. I knew that if they were from the Yemen we should be doomed. Looking back on the journey I realize how hopelessly I under-estimated the danger and how very slight were our chances of survival.

It was midday by now and there was still a crowd of people on the well, which had run dry. We therefore decided to stop to fill our water-skins during the night, and to water our camels at dawn before the Arabs arrived.

In the evening Ali came to our camping place with the two men who had agreed to go with us to the Hassi. They were called Salih and Sadr and were about the same age as Muhammad. They told us that they had been to the Hassi from Najran the year before and were certain that they would be able to find this well as soon as we reached the Aradh, a limestone escarpment running down into the Sands from Sulaiyil. In the evening they went back to their tents, but assured us that they would be with us at dawn.

Sadr had told us that Ibn Saud had a post at the Hassi, and it therefore seemed unlikely that we should be able to water there and slip away again unobserved. I wondered what the King would say when he heard that I had crossed the desert without his permission, and whether he would identify me as the Englishman to whom he had refused permission to do the journey two years before. I only hoped that if we succeeded his anger would be tempered by some admiration for our achievement.

The Second Crossing of the Empty Quarter

The crossing of the Western Sands to the Hassi well and Sulaiyil ends in arrest and imprisonment.

It was a bleak morning with a cold wind blowing from the north-east. The sun rose in a dusty sky but gave no warmth. Bin Kabina set out dates and fragments of bread, left over from the previous night, before calling to us to come and eat. I refused, having no desire for food, and remained where I was, crouching behind a rock, trying to find shelter from the cutting wind and eddies of driven sand. I had slept little the night before, trying to assess the dangers and difficulties which lay ahead. Later, in grey borderlands of sleep, I had struggled knee-deep in shifting sand with nightmares of disaster. Now, in the cold dawn, I questioned my right to take these men who trusted me to what the Saar vowed was certain death. They were already moving about their tasks preparatory to setting off, and only an order from me would stop them. But I was drifting forward, slack-willed, upon a movement which I had started, half-hoping that Salih and Sadr would fail to come and that then we could not start.

Some Saar were already at the well, which would soon be surrounded by Arabs impatient to water their animals. We drove ours down there and filled the troughs, but they would only sniff at the ice-cold water instead of drinking, and drink they must if they were to survive for sixteen waterless days, struggling heavily-loaded through the sands. Bin Kabina and I went back to sort the loads, while the others couched each roaring camel in turn, and, after tying her knees to prevent her from getting up, battled to hold her weaving neck, so that they could pour down her throat the water she did not want.

While we were busy dividing our stores into loads of suitable weight, Salih and Sadr arrived and I was glad to see that both their camels were powerful animals in good condition. We had decided the night before that we would load the spare camels heavily, at the risk of foundering them before we reached the Hassi, so as to save our mounts. I hoped that the two Saar would be able to slip away unobserved from that well, even if the rest of us were detained, and it was therefore important that their camels should be spared as much as possible. They must carry only the lightest loads, if they carried anything at all. I gave them

We had started on our journey, and holding out our hands we said together, 'I commit myself to God'.

Bin Ghabaisha had the rifle I had given him in Saiwun, bin Kabina the one I had given him the year before, and I had my sporting ·303, so we were a well-armed party.

the rifles which I had promised, and fifty rounds of ammunition each. Their friends who had come with them examined these weapons critically, but could find nothing wrong. I had already presented Muhammad and Amair each with a rifle and a hundred rounds of ammunition.

The others returned from the well and we loaded the camels. The sun was warmer now and I felt more cheerful, reassured by the good spirits of my companions, who laughed and joked as they worked. Before leaving, we climbed the rocky hill near the well, and Sadr's uncle, a scrawny old man in a loincloth, showed us once more the direction to follow, pointing with both his arms. With his wild hair, gaunt face, and outstretched arms he looked, I thought, like a prophet predicting doom. I was almost surprised when he said in an ordinary voice that we could not go wrong, as we should have the Aradh escarpment on our left when we reached the Jilida. Standing behind him I took a bearing with my compass.

The camels lurched to their feet as we took hold of the headropes, and, after each of the Rashid had tied a spare camel behind his own, we moved off on foot. Ali came with us a short distance, and then, after embracing each of us in turn, went back.

Two hours later Sadr pointed to the tracks of five camels that had been ridden ahead of us the day before. At first we wondered if they were Yam, but after some discussion Sadr and Salih were convinced that they were Karab and therefore friendly. Muhammad asked me to judge which was the best camel. I pointed at random to a set of tracks and they all laughed and said I had picked out the one which was indubitably the worst. They then started to argue which really was the best. Although they had not seen these camels they could visualize them perfectly. Amair, bin Ghabaisha, and Sadr favoured one camel, Muhammad, bin Kabina, and Salih another. I knew nothing about Sadr and Salih's qualifications, but felt sure that Amair and bin Ghabaisha were right since they were better judges of a camel than Muhammad or bin Kabina. Not all Bedu can guide or track, and Muhammad was surprisingly bad at both. He was widely respected as the son of bin Kalut and was inclined to be self-important in consequence, but really he was the least efficient of my Rashid companions. Bin Ghabaisha was probably the most competent, and the others tended to rely on his judgement, as I did myself. Amair had a thin mouth, hard unsmiling eyes, and a calculating spirit without warmth. I did not like him, but knew that he was competent and reliable. Travelling alone among these Bedu I was completely at their mercy. They could at any time have murdered me, dumped my body in a sand-drift, and gone off with my possessions. Yet so absolute was my faith in them that the thought that they might betray me never crossed my mind.

The following day we rode across gravel steppes which merged imperceptibly into the Sands of the Uruq al Zaza. By midday the north-east wind was blowing in tearing gusts, bitter cold but welcome, as it would wipe out our tracks and secure us from pursuit. We pressed on until night, hoping in vain to find grazing, and then groped about in the dark feeling for firewood. Here it was dangerous to light a fire after dark, but we were too cold and hungry to be cautious. We found a small hollow, lit a fire, and sat gratefully round the flames. At dawn we ate some dates, drank a few drops of coffee, and started off as the sun rose.

It was another cold grey day, but there was no wind. We went on foot for the first hour or two, and then each of us, as he felt inclined, pulled down his camel's head, put a foot on her neck, and was lifted up to within easy reach of the saddle. Muhammad was usually the first to mount and I the last, for the longer I walked the shorter time I should have to ride. The others varied their positions, riding astride or kneeling in the saddle, but I could only ride astride, and as the hours crawled by the saddle edge bit deeper into my thighs.

For the next two days we crossed hard, flat, drab-coloured sands, without grazing, and, consequently, had no reason to stop until evening. On the second day, just after we had unloaded, we saw a bull oryx walking straight towards us. To him we were in the eye of the setting sun and he probably mistook us for others of his kind. As only about three Englishmen have shot an Arabian oryx, I whispered to bin Ghabaisha to let me shoot, while the oryx came steadily on. Now he was only a quarter of a mile away, now three hundred yards, and still he came on. The size of a small donkey — I could see his long straight horns, two feet or more in length, his pure white body,

and the dark markings on his legs and face. He stopped suspiciously less than two hundred yards away. Bin Kabina whispered to me to shoot. Slowly I pressed the trigger. The oryx spun round and galloped off. Muhammad muttered disgustedly, 'A clean miss,' and bin Kabina said loudly, 'If you had let bin Ghabaisha shoot we should have had meat for supper'; all I could say was 'Damn and blast!'

Bin Ghabaisha was certainly the best rider and the best shot, and always graceful in everything he did. He had a quick smile and a gentle manner, but I already suspected that he could be both reckless and ruthless, and I was not surprised when within two years he had become one of the most daring outlaws on the Trucial Coast with a half a dozen blood-feuds on his hands.

For the next three days we rode across sands where there were only occasional *abal* bushes and a few dry tufts of *ailqi* or *qassis*, the remains of vegetation which had grown after rain four years before. We were now in the Qaimiyat, where parallel dune chains ran from north-east to south-west. These dunes were only about a hundred and fifty feet high, but their steep inclines faced towards us, and the successive floundering ascents exhausted our camels, as they had eaten practically nothing for six days. When we left Manwakh they were very fat, and this gave them reserves on which to draw, but their very fatness distressed them in this heavy sand. They were fresh from pasturage and their backs were soft and unaccustomed to the saddle. Now they were heavily-loaded and doing very long marches. We knew that under such conditions they were certain to develop saddle swellings, which would turn all too easily into ulcers. We would gladly have rested them for a day if we could have found grazing and if our water supply had allowed it. The sheepskins, which I had bought in ignorance, sweated very badly, but we had already finished the water that was in them. Even the goatskins had not been long enough in use to become watertight and we were making constant but ineffectual efforts to check the alarming drip. We passed fresh tracks of oryx and of *rim*, the large white gazelle which is found in the Sands, and knew that if we followed these tracks they would lead us to fresh grazing, but we could not afford to lengthen our journey.

In the afternoon of the sixth day the dune chains turned into gentle downs, but we had already climbed over sixteen of them that day and on one of them a baggage camel collapsed, only moving again when we unloaded her. Bin Kabina's camel went lame in the shoulder, and all the others showed signs of exhaustion. I knew that it would be another ten days before we reached the Hassi and I began to wonder if we should get there.

Next morning we came on the fresh tracks of a pelican which had walked in a straight line across the sand. I tried to remember what it said in the Bible about a pelican in the wilderness. Amair told me that five years earlier he had seen several very large white birds near Mughshin, and that they had left tracks like these. While he was describing these birds we topped a rise and saw that the rolling sands ahead of us were green with *qassis*, growing in tasselled tufts a foot high. We unloaded and turned our camels loose. I knew that this grazing was going to make all the difference to our chance of reaching the Hassi, since it would not only satisfy the camels' hunger but would also alleviate their thirst.

We camped on a floor of hard sand in the shelter of a small dune. Two twisted *abal* bushes, one of them with a broken branch drooping to the ground, three clumps of *qassis*, beside which I had placed my saddle-bags, a pile of camel-droppings, and a low bank of sand, marked with a tracery of lizards' tracks, combined with our scattered possessions to become our home.

In the Qaimiyat, where vegetation is rare. The few abal bushes were the results of the rain which had fallen four years before.

There were similar places all around us, but, because bin Ghabaisha happened to call out 'Stop over there' and we had gone where he had directed, this particular spot acquired a temporary significance.

It was a crisp morning with a gentle breeze. A few white cumulus clouds deepened the blueness of a sky no longer tinged with yellow. Muhammad looked critically at the camels as Amair and bin Ghabaisha drove them towards us, and remarked, 'They look better now. God willing they will be able to reach the Hassi. Anyway, we may find more grazing. It looks as if there is a lot in the Sands this year, but it is very scattered.' It only took us ten minutes to load, and as we moved off I thought how pleasant it was to be free from the burden of possessions.

We walked across the red downs, and half an hour later came to the end of the grazing. Sadr told me that we had been camped on its eastern edge and that it only extended for four or five miles to the west. We could easily have missed it. A little later, finding some broken ostrich eggs, bin Kabina and Amair argued whether ostriches were lawful food, a purely academic point since ostriches had been extinct in southern Arabia for more than fifty years, although a few survived until recently in the Wadi Sirham in northern Arabia. When I was in Syria a Bedu told me that the Rualla had shot one there just before the war; it may well have been the last of them. My companions stopped to show me what their tracks looked like, saying that their grandfathers had known these birds. I had seen plenty of the tracks of the African ostrich, a larger bird than the Arabian, in the Sudan, and the copies which Amair made in the sand were correct. It is sad to think that the Arabian oryx and *rim* are also doomed as soon as cars penetrate into the southern desert. Unfortunately oryx prefer the hard, flat sands and gravel plains to the heavy dunes. Since they differ from the four species to be found in Africa, it means that yet another kind of animal will soon be extinct. In Saudi Arabia during the last few years even gazelle have become rare. Hunting-parties scour the plains in cars, returning with lorry-loads of gazelle which they have run down and butchered.

I always thought each camping place distinctive at the time. The curious shape of some sticks beside the fire, a sprinkle of white on golden sand where bin Kabina had spilt flour, a rope lying where a camel had jerked it as she rose, such trifles seemed to distinguish each camp from others, but in fact the differences were too insignificant and the memory of them soon blurred. All but a few tended to become just one of a thousand others.

Every mile or so I checked our course with my compass; it was difficult to hold everything — the compass, notebook, pencil, camel-stick and head-rope, especially when the camel fidgeted. I had dropped my stick for the second time when bin Kabina, who jumped down from his camel to pick it up, said as he handed it back to me, 'Really, Umbarak, this is too much. If I were you I should divorce her as soon as you get back.' The Bedu have a saying that whenever a man drops his stick his wife is being unfaithful.

Next day we travelled across the Jilida plain. Its surface was of coarse sand and fine gravel, covered in places with small angular pebbles, highly polished by the wind. They were of many kinds: I recognized pieces of porphyry, granite, rhyolite, jasper, and limestone. There were occasional ridges, some of them twenty feet in height, of the quartz conglomerate that underlies the gravel surface of the plain, but these were easily avoided. We travelled fast until midday, when we came on grazing and stopped for two hours. I wandered off to a distant ridge, glad to be alone for a while, and sat watching formless shadows dapple an umber-coloured plain where nothing else moved. It was very still, with the silence which we have driven from our world. Then bin Kabina shouted to me and I went back. Coffee was ready. Muhammad said, 'We thought you were going after those oryx'; and when I asked, 'Which oryx?' he stared at me in amazement. I looked where he pointed and saw them at once, eighteen white dots on the dark plain. Bin Kabina said, 'If they had been Arabs you would have sat there, without seeing them, until they came and cut your throat.' Bedu are always observant; even when they are engrossed in an argument their dark, restless eyes notice everything, and their minds record it. They never daydream.

We found no more grazing and camped at last on flat empty sands beyond the Jilida. We passed much oryx spoor, and saw twenty-eight of them during the day. In the afternoon bin Ghabaisha and I stalked three which we saw ahead of us. As we were getting near them I heard someone calling. Looking round I saw Salih hastening towards us. I thought, 'They have seen Arabs and don't want me to shoot.' When he came up he said, 'Look out or you will give them your wind.' I whispered furiously, 'I hunted animals before you were born. It is you who will frighten them by making such a beastly noise.' Whereupon he merely added to my exasperation by maintaining that oryx did not mind the sound of voices, an inexplicable belief held by some of the Bedu, which probably explains why so few of them succeed in shooting one. I had to take a long shot. I saw that I had hit the one I had fired at, but they all galloped off. We hurried forward and found blood-stains on the ground. When the camels arrived we followed the oryx, but they were going to the south-east and after a while the others refused to go on, saying that we could not afford to lengthen our march by going in the wrong direction. This was so obviously true that I was forced to agree.

Two days later we reached the Bani Maradh.

Once across the Bani Maradh we were on the southern edge of the *had* pastures on which the Bedu graze their camels, but ours were too thirsty to eat this plant. At midday we came upon tracks, less than a week old, of Arabs and camels, and from now on two of us scouted continuously ahead. We were

uncomfortably aware that our own tracks would show any Arab that we had come from the south. A very strong north wind added to our discomfort by filling our eyes and ears with sand, without, however, hiding our tracks, which remained clearly visible in the valley-bottoms where the ground was covered with a mosaic of highly polished limestone fragments.

About four o'clock we decided to stop, so that we could cook a meal and put out the fire before dark. Salih remained to keep watch behind us, and we turned eastwards along the top of the next dune instead of crossing it. Half an hour later we unloaded in a hollow in the downs where our camels could graze without showing themselves upon a skyline. Sadr and bin Ghabaisha stood guard while Muhammad herded the camels, and the rest of us gathered wood and baked bread. The sky was overcast and I could see that it was raining heavily to the west.

The next day, wet, cold, and tired, we started early on a cloudy, sunless morning. Later the sun came through and it was very hot, and my thirst grew worse and worse. We passed more fortnight-old tracks of Arabs and their herds. Ahead of us Sadr and bin Ghabaisha scanned each slope and hollow before they signed to come on. The rest of us dragged the trembling camels up the slopes, and held them back as they ploughed down the far side of each dune in cascades of sand. The dunes were now about five hundred feet high and at the western end of each valley we could at last see the dark wall of the Aradh. We stopped after nine hours when the camels could go no farther, again cooking a quick meal before sunset, and eating it in the dark after Sadr, who had been watching our tracks, had joined us. We slept fitfully, jerking to wakefulness whenever a camel stirred. It was fine and clear when we started again at sunrise. Two hours later one of the baggage camels lay down and refused to move, until, at Amair's suggestion, we poured a little water down her nostrils, which revived her. We reached the Aradh at one o'clock and camped two hours later in a shallow watercourse on the limestone plateau. We were across the Sands.

Looking at the mountainous dunes which stretched across our front, I realized that our real difficulties were only now beginning. Fortunately the prevailing winds were different from those in the sands to the south of the Jilida, and in consequence the easier slopes faced south. Even so they imposed a severe strain on our tired camels; they had had only one full meal in the eleven days since we had left Manwakh. If these southern faces had been steep, as in the Uruq al Shaiba the year before, we should never have got over them. Each dune was three to four hundred feet in height, and the highest peaks were built up round deep crescent-shaped hollows. It took us an hour or more to cross each range. Their northern faces fell away in unbroken walls of sand into successive valleys, two miles or more across, which ran down from the Aradh escarpment, and continued until they disappeared from sight twenty miles or more to the east.

Overleaf: So far the sands we had passed on this journey had been dreary and uninteresting. Now for the first time the dunes were a lovely golden-red and, although I was tired, hungry and thirsty, their shapes gave me great pleasure.

We reached the Hassi three days later, after travelling north-ward across a gravel plain scattered with pieces of limestone. It was sixteen days since we had left Manwakh.

Having watered our camels and filled our skins, we learnt from some women that Ibn Saud's guardian on the well had just gone off with his son to look for a strayed camel. Sadr and Salih were anxious to seize this opportunity and slip away before he returned. We loaded their camels with all the food and water that they could carry, and as the women had told us that the Yam had all moved westwards a week ago and that the sands to the south were empty, we hoped that they would be all right. To avoid arousing suspicion we told the women that they were going to fetch one of our camels which had collapsed two days earlier. We whispered our farewells, embraced them, and they left us. They arrived safely at Manwakh, as I later heard from bin al Kamam when I met him on the Trucial Coast.

There was nothing for us now to do but to go to Sulaiyil and hope for the best. Our camels were in need of rest; we had very little food and no guide. Even if we had been able to slip away, a pursuit party would certainly be sent after us. The guardian of the well, a Yam, returned next day and made no attempt to con-ceal his dislike of us. When he learnt that I was a Christian he refused to drink the coffee we offered him, saying that I was an infidel and that my companions, as Muslims who had sold themselves into the service of an infidel for gold, were even worse. Virtually under arrest, we went with him to Sulaiyil, where we arrived two days later. We stopped at the Amir's house, flat-roofed and made of mud, like all the others.

Rather to my surprise, the Amir, who was a young slave, received us graciously. He showed us to an empty house with a courtyard on the outskirts of the village and, after saying that we should of course feed with him, told us that we must remain at Sulaiyil until he heard from Ibn Saud. He and one of his retainers, a Murra who knew the Rashid, and two young wire-less operators were the only friendly people. Everyone else was fanatical and unpleasant. The elders spat on the ground when-ever we passed, and the children followed me round chanting derisively, '*Al Nasrani, al Nasrani,*' the name by which these Arabs know a Christian. When after supper we gave the Amir an account of our journey, he said: 'You do not realize how lucky you have been to get here. I should not have thought that you would have had a chance. The sands you came through were filled with Arabs until a week ago, when most of them moved westward across the Aradh to better grazing. If a single Arab had seen you, the hue-and-cry would have been out, for they would have known at once that you are from the south. Didn't you know that Ibn Saud has given permission to his tribes to raid the Mishqas and to kill any of them they meet, in revenge for the recent raids on the Yam and the Dawasir? They are wildly excited here at having permission to raid after years of enforced peace. He looked at me, shook his head, and said again, 'By God, you were lucky!' I knew he was right and real-ized how badly I had misjudged our chances. This realization increased the responsibility I felt towards my companions.

Two days later the Amir came to our room to tell me he had received orders by wireless from Ibn Saud to detain the Englishman and to imprison his companions. He removed our

rifles and daggers, told me to remain where I was, leaving the Murra as a guard, and ordered Muhammad and Amair to follow him. He said that bin Kabina and bin Ghabaisha, who were herd-ing the camels, could wait till the evening. When I protested at being separated from my companions, and asked that we should be treated alike, he said he must obey the King's orders, but allowed me to send a telegram to Ibn Saud. After several efforts I composed a telegram saying that we had been travelling in the Empty Quarter and had come to the Hassi for water. I asked for his forgiveness, adding that if he wished to punish anyone I was solely to blame, since my companions, who had no knowledge of this country, had gone where I wished and that it was I who had guided them.

In the evening, I saw bin Kabina and bin Ghabaisha com-ing towards the village with the camels. They looked very cheerful, laughing and joking together. The Murra allowed me to meet them and tell them what had happened. Seeing me, some children called out, 'Now the King will cut off the Christian's head and the heads of his companions.' I felt worse about them than I did about the others, for they were so much younger. They asked a few questions, and then bin Kabina put his hand on my shoulder and said, 'Don't worry, Umbarak; if God wills, all will be well.'

At sunset the Amir did his best to cheer us up with a meal in his house, but it was an unhappy evening. Hours later when I was half asleep the door was thrown open. A large black slave came in swinging a pair of fetters, and ordered me to get up and go with him at once, as the Amir of the Wadi had arrived. I fol-lowed through silent streets to the Amir of Sulaiyil's house.

After coffee and tea had been handed round, the Amir of the Wadi said I must go with him to Dam, and that one of my companions could come with me. I asked for bin Kabina. Eventually the two of us climbed into the back of the Amir's truck, the slave who had fetched me from my room got in with us, still holding the fetters. After the Amir, his clerk, and the dri-ver had mounted in front, we drove off to the west. It was very cold, the car lurched and bumped, and bin Kabina was car-sick. He had told me as we waited to get into the car that all four of them had been put in the stocks, when suddenly a messenger arrived and asked which was bin Kabina. I said the Amir had given permission for one of them to accompany me and that I had asked for him. He replied, 'You should have asked for Muhammad. He is the eldest.'

At last we arrived at another village and stopped in front of a large castle. The slave informed us that we were at Dam. We followed the Amir inside, and he gave orders for tea and coffee to be made, and a fire to be lit where we could warm ourselves. He told me that he had seen my telegram to the King, and said, 'Don't worry. I am sure that all will be well.' Then he bade us good night and left the room.

Below the precipitous western edge of the Aradh on the left, were the three shallow wells of Zifr.

The Hassi well, which we reached sixteen days after leaving Manwakh.

From Sulaiyil to Abu Dhabi

After our release we plan to travel eastwards to the Trucial Coast. We visit Laila where we are refused a guide, but make our own way to Abu Dhabi.

The campsite with all we had. We were now only five: bin Kabina, bin Ghabaisha, Muhammad bin Kalut, Amair and myself.

We were in a small bare room at the top of the castle. We had been given bread and tea at dawn, but since then no-one had come near us. It was now nearly eleven o'clock. Bin Kabina, silent and depressed, had covered himself again with his blanket and I wondered if he was asleep.

Finally, the door opened and the Amir came in. Smiling, he said cheerfully, 'I told you it would be all right. Abdullah Philby spoke to the King on your behalf, and the King has given orders that you are to be released and allowed to go on your way.' Philby, who is a Muslim, had lived in Riyadh for many years and was a regular attendant at the King's court. I had seen him recently in London, and had told him that I planned this journey.

The Amir now asked where I proposed to go, so that he could inform the King. I told him that I would like to go to Laila and to cross from there to the Trucial Coast. He said that the car was waiting and would take me back to Sulaiyil.

We went to the Amir of Sulaiyil's house where the others were waiting for us, having spent a cold night in the stocks. Bin Ghabaisha said, 'By God! if I had realized that they were going to do this to me they would never have caught me, when I had a rifle in my hand and a camel under me'; but they were as relieved as I was that nothing more had happened to them. We arranged to go to Laila next day. We had little food left, but agreed that it would be better to buy what we needed there than tire our camels by carrying it.

We left Sulaiyil next morning, 29 January. Laila was a hundred and sixty miles away, and Abu Dhabi on the Trucial Coast was at least six hundred miles beyond that, twice as far from here as Manwakh, from where we had started our journey. It took us eight days to reach Laila. Our camels were tired, and Muhammad's camel and three of the baggage camels had large saddle-swellings. The Amir at Sulaiyil warned us that we should find no grazing other than acacias until near Laila, where there had been a little rain in the autumn.

The first afternoon we overtook two Yam and a Dahm driving a couple of hundred white sheep and black goats to Laila

for sale. We camped with them and bought a goat for our evening meal, which they shared with us. They were friendly, and curious about our journey across the Sands. When we left them they explained how to find the next well. There was a clearly-marked track to Laila, and this route, surveyed by Philby, was shown on the map I had with me.

The last two days before we reached Laila were bitterly cold, with a strong north-easterly wind. We rode across a stony plateau which sloped gently to the east. There was little vegetation until we were near the town, when the ground was suddenly covered with a small white flower called *rahath*. We stopped early, so that the camels could have a good feed, and started late next morning. It was a pleasure to look round at sunset and see our camels lying down fully fed, instead of roaming about in their perpetual hungry quest for food. This was only the second time they had had enough to eat since we had left Manwakh. Little did I know that it was going to take us another forty days to reach Abu Dhabi and that in all that time our camels would only get one more proper meal. After dark we saw the lights of a car in the distance. Later we heard its engine racing and realized that it was stuck in the sand. Resenting all cars, especially in Arabia, I was rather pleased that it was in trouble!

The following afternoon we rode into Laila, a small dun-coloured town of flat-roofed mud buildings, with a population of about four thousand. We halted outside the Amir's house, where we were told by a slave to unload our camels, and were then shown into a long dark room. We greeted the Amir, a sour-faced, elderly man called Fahad, who was wrapped in a gold-embroidered cloak. He called for coffee and tea and then informed me in as few words as possible that Abdullah Philby had arrived yesterday by car from Riyadh, and not finding me here had gone off to look for me.

For the next two hours we sat in silence, which did not, however, prevent the Amir from making it quite clear how greatly he resented my presence.

Philby arrived about an hour later. He was an old friend of mine and I was delighted to see him. His car had stuck in the sands while he was looking for us, and I realized that it was his lights which we had seen the night before. He said: 'I happened to call on the King just after the telegram arrived informing him that you and your party had turned up in Sulaiyil. He was absolutely furious. Asked me if I knew who you were; then said he would make an example of you that would stop other unauthorized Europeans from entering his country. I tried to put in a word for you, but he wouldn't even let me open my mouth. I was worried what might happen to you and decided the best thing to do was to write him a letter. I gave it to him in the morning, saying as I did so that it was a man's duty to intercede for his friends. He was quite different from the night before; said at once that he would send off an order for your release.'

I grumbled about my churlish reception by the Amir that afternoon. Philby was sympathetic, but told me that I ought to realize that as a Christian I was anathema to these strict Wahabis. He pointed out that, after all, it was only this rigid adherence to their principles in a fast changing world that still preserved in a few remote areas the qualities which we both admired in the Arabs. To illustrate the length to which their puritanism sometimes led them, he told me that once he was sitting with Ibn Saud on the palace roof in Riyadh when they heard someone singing in the distance. Genuinely shocked, the King exclaimed, 'God protect me! Who is that singing?' and sent an attendant to fetch the culprit. The man came back with a Bedu boy who had been driving camels into the town. Sternly the King asked the boy if he did not realize that to sing was to succumb to the temptings of the devil, and ordered him to be flogged.

Philby left the next day, but we remained for a further twenty-four hours in Laila, during which time the Amir left us without food. I did not see him again. My Rashid tried to buy supplies for our journey, but were cursed and spat at for bringing an infidel into the town. The shopkeepers said that they would only accept our money after it had been publicly washed. This nicety did not, however, prevent them from charging us exorbitant prices when eventually I got hold of some flour, rice, dates, and butter through the Amir's son. Muhammad asked the Amir to find us a guide to take us to Jabrin, but he answered, 'I will encourage no man to travel with an infidel.'

In the early days of Islam, while their faith was still unchallenged, the Arabs were remarkably tolerant about religion. But to the people of Laila I was an intruder from an alien civilization, which they identified with Christianity. They knew that the Christian had subjugated most of the Muslim world, and that contact with their civilization had everywhere destroyed or profoundly modified the beliefs, institutions, and culture they cherished. Naturally they did not realize how little sympathy I had with the innovations and inventions with which they associated me, nor how much sympathy I had with the way of life they sought to preserve.

In the evening we discussed what we should do. Jabrin was about a hundred and fifty miles away, but I was confident that I could get there by following Philby's route, which was shown on an otherwise blank map. I realized, however, that if I failed to find this oasis we should be lost in the empty waterless desert to the south of the Hasa. I suggested to the others that I should guide them, but they were naturally doubtful of my ability to find a place which I had never seen, and which was eight days' journey away.

I said, 'We don't need a guide, I can find the way.'

Bin Ghabaisha asked. 'How can you do that? You have never seen the country.'

I explained: 'Abdullah Philby marked Jabrin on the map. I can find it with my compass.'

Muhammad was sceptical: 'There are no landmarks. The way is across open plains like the Jaddat al Harasis; it is different from the journey we have just made. Then we did not need a guide. We knew the Aradh was on our left. We had only to strike it to arrive at the Hassi. The Saar knew the actual place of the well. Now we need a guide.'

I suggested that we should probably meet some Bedu on the way, but Amair said doubtfully, 'They say here that the country is empty. There has been no rain.'

I went on, 'Believe me, I can find Jabrin. By God, I don't want to die of thirst in the desert any more than you do!' Bin Kabina asked, 'How many days will it take?' I answered, 'Eight'; and he said: 'That is what they say here.'

Eventually they agreed that I should guide them. Bin Ghabaisha said, 'It is obvious we shall not find a guide here and God forbid we should remain in Laila. We must put ourselves in Umbarak's hands.'

We had left Laila with very little food. Left to right: Amair, bin Ghabaisha, Muhammad and bin Kabina.

I hoped we should find Arabs at Jabrin. By then we should need more food, and, what was far more important, we should need a guide to show us the water-holes on our way to Abu Dhabi, four hundred miles farther on. Without a guide we should be stranded at Jabrin with worn-out camels, in the northern wastes of the Empty Quarter. It was not a pleasant thought.

That evening Muhammad tried to give me some money. He said, 'Abdullah Philby gave us this before he left. Here is a fifth of it, your share; we are travelling companions and should share all things alike.'

We left Laila on 7 February. We carried six skins full of water, and had with us ninety pounds of flour, fifteen pounds of rice, thirty pounds of dates, and some butter, sugar, tea, and coffee. As we were unlikely to get anything but dates from the Murra at Jabrin, I knew that we were going to be very hungry before we reached Abu Dhabi. I reckoned that it would take us at least a month to get there. We therefore decided to ration ourselves to three pounds of flour between the five of us for our one evening meal. We could use the rice only when we were on a well and had plenty of water. We would eat the dates for breakfast, or rather they would, for by now I could no longer even stand the sight of dates. As we led our camels out of the town, some Arabs shouted to us not to come back if we failed to find the way.

My diary shows that it took us eight days to reach Jabrin, and records our marching hours, which were not really long, since only twice did we do eight hours in a day. But my recollection is of riding interminably through a glaring haze-bound wilderness, which seemed to be without beginning and without end. The weariness of our camels added to my own, making it barely tolerable, especially when their bodies jerked in flinching protest as they trod with their worn soles upon the flints which strewed alike the hollows and the ridges. Sometimes we found a path, and its smooth surface afforded them temporary relief, but I dared not follow it if it deviated from my compass course, for there were no landmarks in this desert which I could recognize to warn me if I was going wrong. I knew that I should only have to be eight or ten miles out to miss Jabrin, not much after a hundred and fifty miles. Was Jabrin shown accurately on the map? Though Cheesman and Philby were meticulously accurate in their work, both of them had fixed Jabrin after a long journey.

In the evening we camped wherever we could find a few bushes to give us fuel. We would turn the camels loose to search for food and I would watch them hobbling away, heading back instinctively towards their homelands in the south; and as they got farther and farther away, adding yet more miles to the miles they had already covered that day, I would think wearily, 'Now one of us will have to go and get them.' The weather was very cold, and on most nights we could see lightning and sometimes hear thunder, and I hoped it would not rain, for we would have no sort of shelter.

On previous journeys it had needed a conscious effort on my part to understand what my companions said; but now, although I still spoke Arabic haltingly, for I am a bad linguist, I could no longer withdraw into the sanctuary of my own mind, beyond reach of their disputes. I could follow their talk too easily. For one entire day bin Kabina and Muhammad argued about the money I had given them two years before at Tarim. On the ground that the camel which bin Kabina had ridden belonged to him, Muhammad had kept two-thirds of the money which I had intended for bin Kabina. Remembering how destitute bin Kabina had been at the time, I thought this mean and said so. The argument went on and on, angry shouted interruptions checking but not halting an endless flow of repetition. It only came to an end when we stopped for the night. They then sat contentedly together baking bread. Throughout another day, bin Kabina and Amair wrangled continuously about the respective merits of their grandfathers. Bin Kabina said maliciously, 'Anyway, my grandfather never farted in public,' and the discomfited Amair blushed for this appalling solecism on the part of a grandfather who had been dead for twenty years. When next day they started to quarrel once more about their grandfathers, I protested. They looked at me in surprise and said, 'But it passes the time,' which I suppose was true.

Two days before we reached Jabrin we crossed the Dahana Sands, here about fifteen miles wide. This belt of crescent dunes links the Sands of the Empty Quarter with the great Nafud Sands in northern Arabia. Rain had fallen two months earlier and had penetrated three feet into the Sands, which were touched with a bloom of newly sprung seedlings. To me the unexpected hint of spring in the drab monotony of those days was very welcome. On the eighth morning we climbed a final ridge. I had calculated that if we were ever to see Jabrin we should see it now; and there it lay, straight in front of us, the splashes of the palm-groves dark on the khaki plain. I sat down on a tumulus to rest, for I was very tired, while the others broke into excited talk. Later, we went down into the plain and found a well near a grove of acacias.

We watered the camels and turned them loose. They would no doubt find something, although even the acacias were leafless from the long drought. Only twice during the past eight days had I noticed anything which I thought they could eat, but I suppose they must have found something more during those shuffling quests which took them so far afield. Bin Kabina may have noticed the compassion in my eyes, for he said, 'Their patience is very wonderful. What other creature is as patient as a camel? That is the quality which above all else endears them to us Arabs.'

Bin Kabina.

Muhammad.

The well was shallow and the water sweet. My companions stripped off their shirts and poured buckets of water over each other, but I shrank from this bitter washing in the cold wind despite their gibes and encouragement. 'Come on, Umbarak,' called out bin Ghabaisha, and denied that it was cold, although I could hear him gasp each time Amair threw water over him.

Later, Muhammad and Amair went off to look for the Murra. When they came back at sunset they told us that they had found neither Arabs nor fresh tracks. They asked me how much farther I could guide them. Between here and Abu Dhabi, my map showed only a single well called Dhiby, which Thomas had located at the end of his great journey across the Sands. It was about a hundred and fifty miles away in a depression to the south of the Qatar peninsula. Sixty miles to the east of it were the salt-flats of the Sabkhat Mutti, which, starting on the coast, run southward into the desert.

I told the others that I could take them as far as Sabkhat Mutti, but that I neither knew whether I could find Dhiby well nor whether its water would be drinkable. I vaguely remembered Hamad telling me the year before, when we were in Dhafara, that all the water near the Sabkhat Mutti was brackish. However, Muhammad said that if I could guide as far as the Sabkhat Mutti he could then guide us to Abu Dhabi. I was doubtful about this, but we had to go on, since we should starve if we stayed where we were. The others reassured me by saying that we were certain to encounter some of the Murra before we got to the Sabkhat Mutti.

We decided to fill the ten water-skins which we had with us. This would mean that our baggage camels would again be heavily loaded, but we were quite prepared to sacrifice them in order to save our riding camels and ourselves. Three of them and Muhammad's mount had developed deep, evil-smelling ulcers on their humps and withers, where the saddle-swellings had burst and the skin sloughed away. Amair cut off lumps of mortifying fat and flesh, which he said it was better to remove.

The next day we crossed some salt-flats to the far side of the Jabrin depression, where we found a few bushes which had been touched to life by a shower of rain, and there we stopped to let our camels feed. I was again surprised how local were many of these showers, wetting only a few score acres. In the afternoon we rode across a gravel plain marked with many tracks. Towards evening a grey haze from the north came down, blotting out the emptiness that lay beyond.

Next day we travelled for eight and a half hours until we reached the western edge of the Jaub depression, which I hoped would lead us to Dhiby. It was a burning hot day. For the past ten days clouds had banked up each evening and there had been distant thunder and lightning; now it rained almost continuously for three days and intermittently for the next four, often with thunderstorms, especially at night.

The desolation of the Jalib depression, east of Jabin. As I rode across these interminable naked sands it seemed incredible that in three months' time they would be covered with flowering shrubs.

They were miserable days. It was maddening to ride along drenched to the skin and watch the driving rain soak into the sand, for although I was bitterly cold I was also thirsty. We had no idea where we should find more water, and were again rationing ourselves to a pint a day. We had nothing with us, except a few small pots, in which to catch the rain, not that we could afford the time to stop. My companions were worried about the camels, and warned me that we might wake up any morning and find some of them dead, killed in their weakened state by the ulcers which were eating into them. Each morning I looked anxiously to see if they were still alive.

One night there was a terrific storm, which started soon after dark and revolved around us until dawn. On that bare plain there was no sort of shelter. We could only lie cowering on the ground while the lightning slashed through the darkness of driven clouds, and the thunder crashed about our ears. I had placed my rug and sheepskin over my sleeping-bag. On other nights these had kept me fairly dry, but tonight the weight of water was too great to be turned aside. It flowed over me like an icy torrent.

At dawn there was no wood dry enough to light a fire. We exchanged once more the sodden misery of the night for the cold, dripping discomfort of the day, as we forced the unwilling camels forward into the wind and stinging rain. Nothing grew here but occasional matted growths of salt-bush, whose juicy green foliage gave an irritating illusion of fertility to depressions which were really more sterile than the surrounding sands. That evening the starving camels, finding nothing else, ate these bushes and suffered next day from the inevitable diarrhoea. We tied their tails sideways to our saddlery to prevent them from flicking messily over our clothes. There was no food in their stomachs, but this loss of liquid would entail immediate thirst. Luckily we came on a well, a shallow hole in hard sand, discernible from a distance only by the carpet of camel-droppings that surrounded it. We tasted the water, but it was too brackish to drink; the thirsty camels, however drank as if they could never have enough. While we watered them a gleam of pale sunlight flooded across the wet plain, like slow, sad music. Then it started to rain again. Bin Kabina coaxed a fire to burn, and cooked a large meal of rice in water from the well, but it tasted horrible and most of it remained uneaten. Next day was fine and sunny and our spirits rose as the sun dried our clothes and warmed our bodies. My companions sang.

Eskimos enduring the cold and the darkness of the Arctic winter can count the days till the sun appears, but here in southern Arabia the Bedu have no certainty of spring. Often there is no rain, and even if there is, it may fall at any time of the year. Generally, the bitter winters turn to blazing summers over a parched and lifeless land. Bin Kabina told me now that he only remembered three springs in his life.

Bad days in the Wadi Jalib.

Occasional springtimes such as these were all the Bedu ever knew of the gentleness of life. A few years' relief from the anxiety of want was the most they ever hoped for. It seemed to me pathetically little and yet I knew that magnificently it was enough. As we rode along, the others spoke of years when it had rained, and bin Kabina told me that never in his life had he known such rain as this.

On the afternoon of the eighth day since we had left Jabrin I reckoned that we must be near Dhiby well, and my calculation was confirmed by the bearings which I took on two rocky peaks in a low escarpment to the north of us. An hour later, after again checking our position, I said that we were near the well. Bin Ghabaisha went on to look for it and found it a quarter of a mile away in a hollow in the sands. He came back and said, 'By God, Umbarak, you *are* a guide!', but my justifiable satisfaction was spoilt when the water proved too brackish to drink. The camels, however, were thirsty and drank it greedily.

Near the well there was a little fresh *qassis* which I hoped foretold that we were on the edge of grazing, but the next day we marched twenty-eight miles and found nothing all day. It rained again throughout the night. I was too cold and wet to sleep, too worried about what we should do.

After the heavy rains, the sands looked as if they had been uncovered by an outgoing tide. It had rained, not scattered showers, but downpours which might well have covered all the desert. 'God's bounty' my companions called it, and rejoiced at the prospect of rich grazing that would last for years.

We had decided to go on to the Sabkhat Mutti, still hoping to find Arabs, but as we had found no trace of any so far I saw no reason why we should. My map marked only Abu Dhabi about two hundred and fifty miles farther on and our water was nearly finished.

We woke to a grey, lowering day, heavy with massed clouds, threatening rain. With cold, numbed fingers we loaded our camels and then walked dispiritedly beside them trying to bring some warmth into our bodies, while our long shirts flapped damply round our legs. I felt sure that the camels could not survive another day. Then unbelievably we came on grazing. It covered only a few square miles, and we walked straight into it. The camels hardly moved. They just ate and ate. We stood and watched them and bin Ghabaisha said to me, 'This grazing has saved our lives.'

Next day we crossed the Sabkhat Mutti. We decided we must make a detour and cross these salt-flats near their head, otherwise the camels might become inextricably bogged, especially after the recent heavy rain. They would only have to sink in as far as their knees to be lost. Camels are always bad on greasy surfaces, so we fastened knotted cords under their feet to stop them from slipping. Here the salt-flats were divided into three arms by crescent-patterned drifts of sterile white sand. The flats themselves were covered with a crust of dirty salt which threw up a glare into our faces and, even through half-closed eyes, stabbed deep into my skull. The camels broke through this crust and floundered forward through liquid black mud. It took us five unpleasant, anxious hours to get across.

On the far side we camped among undulating, utterly lifeless white sands, where even the salt-bushes were dead and their stumps punctured our naked feet like needles. It was eleven days since we had left Jabrin. In the evening we had a long and anxious discussion. Muhammad had at last to admit that he knew nothing about this country, and my map was a blank as far as Abu Dhabi, which was still two hundred miles away. We had only a few gallons of water left. We should never get there unless we found water, and none of us had any idea if there were any wells along the coast. Muhammad said that we should probably find Bedu. He had been saying this since we left Laila, and we had come three hundred and fifty miles without meeting any. Finally, in desperation, I suggested that we should try to find the Liwa oasis, which I reckoned was only about a hundred miles away. I had not yet been there, but bin Kabina had visited three of the settlements from Balagh well when he fetched food for us the year before. He agreed that he would recognize the shape of the dunes at Liwa if I could guide us there. Unfortunately I did not have with me the compass-traverse which I had then made. Liwa was written in large letters across the map, but it was marked from hearsay, for no European other than myself had been near there. I puzzled over this map. Each time I fixed a bearing, some reason or other

In the Dhafara.

made me think I was wrong. The others sat round and watched me as I worked in the failing light. We all knew that if I went wrong and we missed Liwa we should be heading back into the Empty Quarter. It was a frightening thought; but to look for Liwa seemed to be our only chance. Next morning, after travelling for twelve miles across flat white sands, we came to a succession of dune-chains, each of which, when approached from the west, showed up in turn as a wavy silver-blue wall, three to four feet high, running out of sight to north and south along the top of an orange-red slope a mile wide. Their farther sides fell away into a jumble of hollows. They gradually became larger and more complicated and developed into high but uniform dune-ranges and swelling downs, full of crescent-shaped hollows and deep pot-holes. The steeper sides of many of these hollows showed marks where water from the recent heavy rain had flowed down, and in some places the crust formed by the rain had been pitted by hailstones. Here we found grazing and noticed the tracks of hares, fennec foxes, honey badgers, and monitor lizards. On 28 February we found a filled-in well at the bottom of a deep hollow. Bin Kabina climbed to a summit and shouted down to us, 'I can see the Sands of Liwa.' We climbed up to join him, and I saw the great mountains of golden sand where we had been the year before. We were safe now, but no one commented on the fact. Muhammed merely said, 'Those dunes are rather like those in Ghanim.'

The Dhiby well, where we found a little grazing for our camels.

We arrived at Balagh on 4 March, passing the hollow where bin Kabina and I had camped and starved for three days on our last journey. It was a still, hot afternoon. Next morning we found a small Manasir encampment on the edge of Liwa, and persuaded a man to guide us to Abu Dhabi.

We were now on the western edge of Liwa, which our guide said extended eastward for three days' journey. I should have liked to explore this famous oasis, but our camels were exhausted and we ourselves were worn out. Our food was nearly finished and it was difficult to buy anything here but dates. I knew that we must go direct to Abu Dhabi, and could only hope that perhaps I should be able to come back later.

The Arabs here were Bani Yas. They lived in rectangular cabins made from palm fronds, built for the sake of coolness on the downs above the palm groves, two or three cabins being enclosed by a high fence and inhabited by one family. They owned some camels and a few donkeys and goats, and in the summer many of them went to Abu Dhabi to join the pearling fleet as divers.

We left Liwa on 7 March. Abu Dhabi was still a hundred and fifty miles away, but now we had a guide. We were very tired, and were no longer sustained by the struggle to survive, so each day's march became a plodding weariness during which we were inclined to quarrel over trifles. It rained at intervals during these days, sometimes heavily.

We reached the coast and followed it eastward through desolate country. There were limestone ridges, drifts of white sand, and stretches of gravel dotted with tussocks of woody grass and shrivelled plants.

The scene was colourless, without tones or contrast. We descended to the salt-flats that ran out far to sea, and led our slithering camels across this greasy surface to the creek which separates Abu Dhabi from the mainland. It was 14 March. We had left Manwakh on 6 January.

A large castle dominated the small town which stretched along the shore. There were a few palms, and near them was a well where we watered our camels while some Arabs eyed us curiously, wondering who we were. Then we went over to the castle and sat outside the walls, waiting for the Sheikhs to wake from their afternoon slumbers.

We led our camels to the creek which separates Abu Dhabi from the mainland. We waded through the sea, rested for a while outside the stone fort which guards the ford, and then went on to the town.

The Trucial Coast

From Abu Dhabi we go to Buraimi where we stay for a month with Zayid bin Sultan, and then travel to Sharja. From Dibai I sail by dhow to Bahrain.

Shakhbut (to my left) and Hiza (to my right) were dressed in Saudi fashion, in long white shirts, gold-embroidered cloaks, and white head-cloths, which fell round their faces and were held in place with black woollen head-ropes. Shakhbut's dagger was ornamented with gold.

The castle gates were shut and barred and no one was about. We unloaded our camels and lay down to sleep in the shadow of the wall. Near us some small cannon were half buried in the sand. The ground around was dirty, covered with the refuse of sedentary humanity. The Arabs who had watched us watering had disappeared. Kites wheeled against a yellow sky above a clump of tattered palms, and two dogs copulated near the wall.

In the evening a young Arab came out from a postern gate, walked a little way across the sand, squatted down, and urinated. When he had finished, Muhammad called to him and asked if the Sheikhs were 'sitting' — an Arab expression for giving audience. The boy answered, 'No, not yet,' and Muhammad told him to tell them that an Englishman had arrived from the Hadhramaut and was waiting to see them. The boy asked, 'Where is the Englishman?' and Muhammad pointed to me and said, 'That's him.'

Half an hour later a grey-bearded Arab came out, asked us a few questions, and went back into the castle. He came out again a little later and invited us in. He led us up some stairs to a small, carpeted room where Shakhbut, the ruler of Abu Dhabi, and his brothers Hiza and Khalid were sitting. They rose as we came in, and after we had greeted them and shaken hands, Shakhbut invited us to be seated.

Shakhbut called for coffee, and it was produced by an attendant in a saffron-coloured shirt. After we had drunk it and eaten a few dates, Shakhbut asked about our journey. Later I mentioned that I visited the outskirts of Liwa the year before. Hiza said, 'We heard rumours from some Awamir that a Christian had been there, but we disbelieved them. We could not believe that a European could have come and gone without being seen. Bedu news, as you know, is often unreliable. We thought they must have been talking of Thomas, who crossed the Sands sixteen years ago.'

Later the Sheikhs escorted us to a large dilapidated house near the market. We climbed up a rickety staircase to a bare room, carpeted ready for our arrival. Shakhbut ordered two of

Shakhbut was a pale, slightly-built man, with small, regular features, a carefully-trimmed black beard, and large dark eyes. He was courteous, even friendly, but aloof. He spoke softly, moved slowly and deliberately, and seemed to impose a rigid restraint on a naturally excitable temper.

his attendants to look after us, and then said that he would leave us now as we must be tired, but would come and see us in the morning. When I asked him about our camels, he said they would be taken into the desert where there was grazing and brought back when we required them; but, he added, that would not be for many days, for we had come a long way and now we must rest here in comfort. He smiled at me and said, 'This is your home for as long as you will stay with us.'

Merchants from the market-place and Bedu who were visiting the town came in to hear our news. A hurricane-lamp smoked through a broken glass but gave some light. It was cosy and very friendly, and pleasing to feel that for a while we had no further need of travelling, that we could eat and sleep at will. I wondered why people ever cluttered up their rooms with furniture, for this bare simplicity seemed to me infinitely preferable.

Overleaf: Every day while in Abu Dhabi we would wander along the beach and watch the dhows being caulked and treated with shark-oil to prepare them for the pearling season, the children bathing in the surf, and the fishermen landing their catch. Once they brought in a young dugong or sea-cow which they had caught in their nets. It was about four feet long, a pathetically helpless-looking creature, hideously ugly. They said its meat was good eating, and that its skin made sandals.

We stayed for twenty days at Abu Dhabi. Each morning the Sheikhs visited us, walking slowly across from the castle — Shakhbut, a stately figure in a black cloak, a little ahead of his brothers, followed by a throng of armed retainers. We talked for an hour or more, drinking coffee and eating sweets, and, after they had left us, we visited the market, where we sat cross-legged in the small shops, gossiping and drinking more coffee.

I was anxious to penetrate into Oman and to visit the places which Staiyun had described to me the year before while we waited in the Wadi al Ain for the others to come back from Ibri. I believed that my best chance of getting there would be from Buraimi, and I hoped that Zayid bin Sultan, Shakhbut's brother, would be able to help me. It was too late in the season to attempt a journey into Oman that year, and anyway I needed a rest. My mind was taut with the strain of living too long among Arabs. But I could at least go up to Buraimi, and make some discreet enquiries about Oman.

I left Abu Dhabi with my four Rashid, and a guide provided by Shakhbut on 2 April. Buraimi was about a hundred miles away, and it took us four days to get there. We had plenty of food and were no longer tired, and there was good grazing. Hiza had lent me a splendid camel to ride. These Al bu Falah sheikhs owned many thoroughbreds from Oman. The Arabs in Abu Dhabi had been inclined to disparage our animals, contrasting them with those owned by their sheikhs, until bin Ghabaisha was provoked to say, 'Your Sheikh's camels are admittedly wonderful animals, pictures of beauty. I am a Bedu, I can appreciate them; but there is not one of them that would do the journey ours have just done,' and his listeners were silent, for there was truth in what the indignant boy said.

The evening before we reached Buraimi I was lying contentedly on the ground watching bin Kabina roasting some toadstools that he had found while herding the camels. They were creamy-tasting and delicious. There were also truffles here which were even better. Bin Ghabaisha tickled my foot, and, instinctively kicking out and catching him in the solar plexus, I knocked him out. Anxiously I bent over him, but bin Kabina said, 'He is all right. He is only knocked out'; and a few seconds later bin Ghabaisha sat up. He said reproachfully, 'Why do you try to kill your brother?' and when I protested he laughed and said, 'Don't be silly; of course I realize it was an accident.' I asked bin Kabina, 'What would you have done if I really had killed bin Ghabaisha?' and he answered at once, 'I should have killed you.' When I protested that it would have been an accident, he said grimly, 'That would have made no difference.' He was joking, and yet I knew that Bedu demand a life for a life whether the killing was intentional or accidental. Sometimes when their temper has cooled they may agree to accept blood-money, especially if the killing was accidental, but their immediate reaction is to exact vengeance.

Next morning we approached Muwaiqih, one of eight small villages in the Buraimi oasis. It was here that Zayid lived.

Abu Dhabi then was a small town of about two thousand inhabitants.

As we came out of the red dunes on to a gravel plain I could see Zayid's fort, a large square enclosure, of which the mud walls were ten feet high. To the right of the fort, behind a crumbling wall half buried in drifts of sand, was a garden of dusty, ragged palm-trees.

Some thirty Arabs were sitting under a thorn-tree in front of the fort. Our guide pointed and said to me, 'The Sheikh is sitting.' We couched our camels about thirty yards away and walked over, carrying our rifles and camel-sticks. I greeted them and exchanged the news with Zayid. He was a powerfully built man of about thirty with a brown beard. He had a strong, intelligent face, with steady, observant eyes, and his manner was quiet but masterful. He was dressed, very simply, in a beige-coloured shirt of Omani cloth, and a waistcoat which he wore unbuttoned. He was distinguished from his companions by his black head-rope, and the way in which he wore his head-cloth, falling about his shoulders instead of twisted round his head in the local manner. He wore a dagger and cartridge-belt; his rifle lay on the sand beside him.

A servant brought rugs for us to sit on; Zayid had been sitting on the bare sand. The servant then produced the inevitable coffee and dates. Zayid asked me questions about my journey, about the distances and the wells we had used, about Jabrin, and the Saudis we had met in Laila and Sulaiyil. He was well informed about the desert, and especially interested when I told him that I had been through the Duru country the year before, and expressed his surprise that the Duru had allowed me to pass. I told him that I had pretended to be a Syrian merchant, and he said laughingly, 'I should have known at once that you weren't.' He mentioned that an Englishman called Bird was staying in Buraimi in another of the villages, trying to persuade the tribes to let a Company look for oil. I gathered that he was having little success.

I had met Dick Bird three years before when he was a Political Officer in Bahrain. He was interested in and sympathetically disposed towards the Arabs, and we later became friends. But I realized that if, in the eyes of the local tribesmen, I became identified with an oil company, it would greatly lessen my chances of getting into Oman, and I therefore decided to stay with Zayid, and not with Bird, while I was in Buraimi.

I stayed with Zayid for nearly a month.

In the mornings, after we had breakfasted on tea and bread, a servant would come in and tell us that the Sheikh was 'sitting'. We would go out and join him. Sometimes Zayid would be on the bench in the porch, but more often under a tree outside the fort. He would call for coffee and we would sit there chatting till lunch-time, though we were frequently interrupted. Visitors would arrive, Bedu from the Sands or from Saudi Arabia, tribesmen from Oman, or perhaps a messenger from Shakhbut in Abu Dhabi. Everyone rose as they approached, and then Zayid would invite them to be seated and listen to their news. As they approached I tried to guess where they came from, noting the way they wore their clothes and saddled their camels. Sometimes they were Rashid or Awamir, and then, sitting beside my companions, they asked news of their kinsmen in the south. They were different from the Bani Yas and Manasir who comprised most of Zayid's retainers, hardier and more refined.

Perhaps an Arab would get up from the circle, sit down immediately in front of Zayid, hit the ground a wallop with his stick to attract attention, and interrupting us as we spoke together, would say: 'Now Zayid, what about those camels which were taken from me?' Zayid, who might be in the middle of a sentence, would stop and listen to the man's complaint. Most of the complaints were about camels. Frequently the complainant averred that some notorious outlaw, who might well be sitting with us, had taken his animals. Zayid had many of these outlaws in his entourage, since it suited him better to have them with him than in some rival sheikh's fort. Bin Ghabaisha, who sat beside me with his rifle between his knees—he was never parted from it—was soon to be numbered among them. I watched him listening with interest as each case was heard. Both sides argued noisily and with frequent interruptions, as was their wont. Zayid had no desire to offend the outlaw, nor to lose his reputation for justice. It was a proof of his skill that he usually satisfied both sides by his judgement.

I remember on one occasion a woman had run away from her husband, and her brothers were anxious that he should divorce her. The husband said that he would only do so if her family returned the full bride-price. This, they argued, was unfair as she had lived with him for years. Zayid consulted some of the greybeards who sat with us, and declared that the family should return half the bride-price. On another occasion a Manasir had shot his sister; we had heard the shot while we were sitting in our room. We soon learnt that she had been seduced by one of Zayid's Bani Yas retainers. Everyone, except my Rashid, thought that her brother had done right. Bin Kabina said to me, 'Poor little girl! It was a brutal thing to kill her.' Next day Zayid sentenced the man who had seduced her to be flogged.

Zayid, as Shakhbut's representative, controlled six of the villages in Buraimi. The other two acknowledged the Sultan of Muscat as their nominal overlord, as did the tribes who lived in and around the mountains northwards from Ibri to the Musandam peninsula, although in fact this area was independent tribal territory.

Each of the Trucial Sheikhs had a band of armed retainers recruited from the tribes, but only Shakhbut had any authority among the tribes themselves, and he maintained this authority by diplomacy, not by force. There was no regular force anywhere on the Trucial Coast nor in Buraimi which could be used to support the authority of the Sheikhs. The Trucial Oman Scouts had not yet been raised, and although the R.A.F. had an aerodrome at Sharja it was only a staging-post on the route to India.

Zayid was often busy during these days helping Bird with his interminable discussions with tribal sheikhs from the surrounding country. Bird used to come over to Muwaiqih in his car — Zayid also had a car and these were the only two nearer than Dibai on the coast. Bird was friendly but suspicious, wondering if I was working for some rival company. I kept away from him when visiting tribesmen were about. Anyway, I was averse to all oil companies, dreading the changes and disintegration of society which they inevitably caused.

> I had been looking forward to meeting Zayid, for he had a great reputation among the Bedu. They liked him for his easy informal ways and his friendliness, and they respected his force of character, his shrewdness, and his physical strength. They said admiringly, 'Zayid is a Bedu. He knows about camels, can ride like one of us, can shoot, and knows how to fight.'

The Iraq Petroleum Company had signed agreements with the Sultan of Muscat and with the Trucial Sheikhs, covering the area round Buraimi, and Bird was now trying to persuade the tribes to accept these agreements. It was not easy, since Zayid had no authority south of Buraimi, and the Sultan, whose authority there was at this time purely nominal, had no effective representative in the area. Each sheikh, excited by avarice, was noisily asserting his independence, while each of his tribesmen fancied that he could get special terms for himself by refusing to acknowledge any authority other than his own. None of this helped my chances of getting into Oman, which seemed slight enough at the best of times.

The interior of Oman had remained one of the least known of the inhabited places of the East, even less well-known than Tibet. It was first visited by Wellsted in 1835, and he was followed two years later by the French botanist Aucher Eloy. Colonel Miles made two long journeys through the country in 1876 and 1885, while he was British Consul in Muscat, and in 1901 Sir Percy Cox travelled southward from Buraimi to Nazwa and then on to Muscat.

I told Zayid of my plans and he promised to help me when I came back in the autumn. He warned me, however, to speak

Bin Kabina on Jabal Hafit, where we camped for a week.

of them to no-one else. I did not even tell my Rashid, for I had learnt that the most effective way to spread a story was to tell it to one or two Arabs under a pledge of secrecy. Zayid offered to send me down to the coast in his car, but I said I would go by camel. This would postpone a little longer my parting with my companions. He then said that he would lend me Ghazala, 'the gazelle', and this delighted me, for she was the most renowned camel in Oman, and may well have been the finest in all Arabia. Muhammad said to me, 'Any Bedu would give much to say that he had ridden Ghazala.'

We left Muwaiqih on 1 May, accompanied by four of Zayid's retainers, for we should pass through Bani Kitab territory and this tribe was at war with Rashid. We rode northwards along the edge of the Sands, parallel with the mountains. It was attractive country. Many watercourses ran down from the foothills and ended in the Sands. They were filled with *ghaf* and acacias which gave food to our camels, and to us shelter from the sun. Already the weather was hot. We dawdled along, for I was reluctant to arrive at Sharja. Bin Ghabaisha and I hunted wild ass, and shot two of them. They looked very different from the graceful, spirited animals I had seen in the Danakil country, and they were later identified as feral donkeys by the British Museum. They were difficult to skin, for our daggers were blunt. It was midday and the sun was very hot, there was no shade on the stony plain where we had found these donkeys, and we had no water with us.

While I had been at Muwaiqih I had hunted tahr on Jabal Hafit, camping for a week under the mountain with bin Kabina and bin Ghabaisha and two of Zayid's Arabs. The Arabian tahr had never previously been seen by a European, although they had been named from two skins bought in Muscat by Dr Jayakar in 1892. They resembled goats and had very thick short horns. It was exhausting work hunting them. The tahr fed at night round the foot of the mountain, but the only ones we saw were near the top. The Arabs shot two females and we picked up the skull of a male.

We arrived at Sharja on 10 May. I stayed with Noel Jackson, the Political Officer on the Trucial Coast, in the peaceful comfort of his rooms. Later he took me round to the R.A.F. mess. Listening to their talk while a wireless blared in a corner and the barman served drinks, I realized that these officers could have as little understanding of Bedu life as bin Kabina or bin Ghabaisha had of theirs. I could now move without effort from one world to the other as easily as I could change my clothes, but I appreciated that I was in danger of belonging to neither.

I said good-bye to my companions at Sharja, hoping to be with them again in four months' time. I then went to Dibai and stayed with Edward Henderson. We had been together in Syria during the war. He was now working for the Iraq Petroleum Company, making preparations for the development which was expected there, but of which there was mercifully as yet no sign. He lived in a large Arab house overlooking the creek which divided the town, the largest on the Trucial Coast with about twenty-five thousand inhabitants.

Many native craft were anchored in the creek or were careened on the mud along the waterfront. There were booms from Kuwait, sambuks from Sur, jaulbauts; to the English all these vessels were dhows, a name no longer remembered by the Arabs.

Rowing-boats patrolled the creek to pick up passengers from the mouths of alleys between high coral houses. Behind the diversity of houses which lined the waterfront were the suqs, covered passage-ways, where merchants sat in the gloom, cross-legged in narrow alcoves among their piled merchandise. The suqs were crowded with many races — pallid Arab townsmen; armed Bedu, quick-eyed and imperious; Negro slaves; Baluchis, Persians, and Indians. Among them I noticed a group of Kashgai tribesmen in their distinctive felt caps, and some Somalis off a sambuk from Aden. Here life moved in time with the past. These people still valued leisure and courtesy and conversation.

I could have gone to Bahrain by aeroplane from Sharja but I preferred to go there by dhow. While waiting for the wind to shift, we were joined by seven other dhows, great ocean-going *booms*, sailing back from Zanzibar to Kuwait. Their *naukhadas* rowed over to visit us, and we fed them on rice and dates and a large fish which we had just harpooned. They drank tea, smoked in turn from a hubble-bubble, and described their voyage, but I found it difficult to follow their talk, for I did not know the terms they used. Then the wind changed and we sailed for Bahrain. It was thrilling to watch these great dhows surging along beside us through the breaking seas.

I was sailing on this dhow because I wanted to have some experience of the Arab as a sailor. Once they had been a great sea-going race, sailing their dhows round the coast of India to the East Indies and perhaps even farther. The Trucial Coast which we had just left had been known and dreaded as the Pirate Coast; in the early nineteenth century pirates had fought our frigates on level terms on these very waters. But there was a deeper reason that had prompted me to make this journey. I had done it to escape a little longer from the machines which dominated our world. The experience would last longer than the few days I spent on the journey. All my life I had hated machines. I could remember how bitterly at school I had resented reading the news that someone had flown across the Atlantic or travelled through the Sahara in a car. I had realized even then that the speed and ease of mechanical transport must rob the world of all diversity.

For me, exploration was a personal venture. I did not go to the Arabian desert to collect plants nor to make a map; such things were incidental. At heart I knew that to write or even to talk of my travels was to tarnish the achievement. I went there to find peace in the hardship of desert travel and the company of desert peoples. I set myself a goal on these journeys, and, although the goal itself was unimportant, its attainment had to

The dhow journey from Sharja to Bahrain should have taken four days but lasted eleven. The naukhada, or skipper, was an old man, nearly blind, who spent most of his time asleep on the poop. The mate, an energetic Negro, described what he saw and the naukhada told him where to go. Once he woke the old man in the middle of the night to consult him. The naukhada gave his orders, but when the mate said 'Nonsense, Uncle!', he went grumbling back to sleep. The first night it blew a gale. The seas broke over the ship and I was very sick. We had to shelter under the Persian coast, and there we remained for three days, since the wind, when it moderated, was against us.

be worth every effort and sacrifice. Scott had gone to the South Pole in order to stand for a few minutes on one particular and almost inaccessible spot on the earth's surface. He and his companions died on their way back, but even as they were dying he never doubted that the journey had been worth while. Everyone knew that there was nothing to be found on the top of Everest, but even in this materialistic age few people asked, 'What point is there in climbing Everest? What good will it do anyone when they get there?' They recognized that even today there are experiences that do not need to be justified in terms of material profit.

No, it is not the goal but the way there that matters, and the harder the way the more worth while the journey. Who, after all, would dispute that it is more satisfying to climb to the top of a mountain than to go there in a funicular railway? Perhaps this was one reason why I resented modern inventions; they made the road too easy. I felt instinctively that it was better to fail on Everest without oxygen than to attain the summit with its use.

Yet to refuse mechanical aids as unsporting reduced exploration to the level of a sport, like big-game shooting in Kenya when the hunter is allowed to drive up to within sight of the animal but must get out of the car to shoot it. I would not myself have wished to cross the Empty Quarter in a car. Luckily this was impossible when I did my journeys, for to have done the journey on a camel when I could have done it in a car would have turned the venture into a stunt.

At last a puff of wind stirred the water and did not immediately die away. The mate shouted to the sleeping crew. They trimmed the sail, stamping and singing as they hauled. The breeze freshened.

We arrived at Bahrain on 28 May, the old blind *naukhada* taking his boat into the crowded roadstead under full sail. She smashed through the choppy waves and brought up within twenty yards of a dhow that had lain beside us under the Persian shore a week before.

Dhows were the last trading vessels in the world that made long voyages entirely by sail. Soon they too would disappear.

A Holiday in Buraimi

I return to Buraimi, visit the Liwa oasis, and go hawking with Zayid

I returned to Dibai from England at the end of October. Musallim bin al Kamam was waiting for me at Henderson's house, having come there to join me from the Yemen, where he had renewed the truce between the Rashid and the Dahm for another two years. He told me how the Imam of the Yemen's son had sent two parties of Dahm to intercept us when we crossed the Sands to Sulaiyil. He said, 'When I reached Najran I heard that you had been imprisoned in Sulaiyil. Bin Madhi, the Amir with whom you once stayed in Najran, declared that you had been lucky to get there, as the Yam would certainly have killed you if they had found you in the Sands.' I was delighted to have bin al Kamam with me, for I had found him amusing and accommodating when he had travelled with me to Tarim. He was exceptionally intelligent, level-headed, and reliable; he had travelled widely, was a good guide, skilled in negotiations, and had considerable authority among the desert tribes.

We left Dibai for Abu Dhabi on 27 October, going there by launch. I had meant to leave for Buraimi on the 31st but it poured with rain during the night and we woke to find most of the island under water. Shakhbut advised us to remain at Abu Dhabi for at least another day, to give the salt-flats, which we had to cross, a chance to dry. So bin al Kamam and I left on 1 November, riding borrowed camels, and arrived at Muwaiqih four days later. Zayid was there and put us in the room that I had been in before. He said, 'Bin Kabina, bin Ghabaisha, and Amair spent last night in an Awamir encampment on the edge of the Sands. They will turn up as soon as they hear that you are here. Muhammad has gone to Dakaka. They've been having a fine time while you were away, lifting camels from everybody.'

It was late at night when they arrived. Bin al Kamam and I had lain down to sleep, when someone hammered at our door and bin Kabina and the other two came in. Bin Kabina said, 'We only just heard that you had arrived. We were off in the morning to raid the Bani Kitab.' We relit the fire, bin al Kamam made coffee, and the others fetched their saddlebags. They asked bin al Kamam about their families and friends, and

Abu Dhabi, where I stayed waiting for the salt-flats to dry after torrential rains.

pressed him for every detail of recent happenings in the south, discussing them at length. Later they told us of their own doings. They had spent the summer harrying the Bani Kitab and other tribes, and serving as soldiers of fortune with the local sheikhs. As I listened to their talk I thought how well their adventures illustrated the chronic insecurity of these parts, where jealous and often hostile sheikhs relied on the uncertain support of the Bedu to maintain their position. These sheikhs competed for the support of the tribesmen by the lavishness of their hospitality and the scale of their gifts. Not one of them was prepared to acknowledge a paramount power, nor were any of them able to enforce their authority over the Bedu; none would even try, lest by doing so they should alienate Bedu support in time of need. In consequence the country was full of outlaws, who feared no punishment other than the blood-feud and the retaliation of hostile tribesmen. Knowing perfectly well that each sheikh would rather have their friendship than incur their enmity, the outlaws travelled quite openly among the villages which they had robbed, assured of hospitality commensurate with the strength and nearness of their own tribe and the reputation which they personally had acquired. If an exasperated ruler did detain them, they knew they could count on an immediate demand for their release by some other sheikh, who, anxious to court their favour, would claim that they were under his protection.

I was anxious to explore Liwa before I started on my journey into Oman. Zayid advised me to take an old Rashid called bin Tahi as my guide. He said: 'You will like him. He is a pleasant old man. He has settled down and become respectable in the last few years, but he was a notorious outlaw when he was younger. He must have lifted camels from pretty well every tribe in southern Arabia, and knows every corner and water-hole in the desert. Your lads know him; everyone does.' Later I asked bin Kabina about bin Tahi and he said, 'Yes, that is a splendid idea. Let's take bin Tahi. He is camped at present near the southern end of Jabal Hafit.' Bin Tahi agreed at once to come with us.

We left Muwaiqih on 14 November and spent about a month travelling through Liwa as far as Dhafara, where we had been the year before. It was a pleasant journey. The Sands were like a garden. There were matted clumps of tribulus, three feet high, their dark green fronds covered with bright yellow flowers, bunches of *karia*, a species of heliotrope, that was rated high as camel-food by the Bedu, and *qassis*, as well as numerous other plants which the camels scorned in the plenty that surrounded them.

Two days later, we camped near a well named Faswat at Ajuz. In the morning Salih and his son, two Rashid who accompanied us on this journey, went on ahead, while the others drove the camels off to water them at the well, out of sight from where I was sitting among our scattered kit writing up my diary. Suddenly I heard a shot and shouts of 'Raiders! Raiders!' Salih and his son raced back over the dunes, shouting as they came towards me. Immediately afterwards the others arrived from the well. They were naked except for their loin-cloths, cartridge-belts, and daggers. Bin Kabina slid from his camel and couched mine. 'Quick, Umbarak! Jump on her.' I turned to get my saddle-bags but bin Kabina urged me, 'Hurry! Hurry!' so I just grabbed a blanket, threw it over the saddle, and mounted. The others were already off. I had no idea whether we were running away or what we were doing. I shouted at bin Kabina to ask him, but like the others he was too excited to be coherent. Anyway, I was finding it difficult to stay on my camel, which had started to gallop, wrenching every joint in my body. I got her under control, and the others slowed theirs to a fast trot. Salih said, 'There are four of them, with eight stolen camels. Without a doubt they are Bani Kitab who have been raiding the Rashid in Dhafara.'

Five minutes later we picked up their tracks. They were travelling fast, but handicapped by the looted animals they were driving. Bin al Kamam said grimly, 'They cannot get away'; and bin Ghabaisha called out, 'We will kill the lot. God's curse on the Bani Kitab.' Bin Tahi was waving his stick and shouting, 'If I had a rifle you would see how bin Tahi fights.' The old man was armed only with a dagger. Bin al Kamam said to me, 'They will head back to the north. You and I and bin Tahi will follow their tracks. The others will try to cut them off.' Bin Kabina called out, 'Don't miss, Umbarak!' as he swung off to the left with bin Ghabaisha, Amair, and Salih.

Two hours later bin Tahi said, 'They are getting tired. Do you notice how that camel is stumbling.' I hoped the others were not far away. Bin Tahi had no rifle and I knew that bin al Kamam's old Martini usually jammed after a shot or two. Then the tracks which we were following turned sharply to the east and bin al Kamam said, 'They have seen our companions. I hope to God they have seen them.' A little later we saw the raiders. They were about a mile away, four mounted figures driving a bunch of camels in front of them. We urged our camels forward and gained rapidly on them. They drove their camels into a hollow and did not reappear on the farther slopes. Bin Tahi said, 'They have stopped. Get off and get up there where you can cover them with your rifles, and then I will go forward and find out who they are.'

Bin al Kamam and I couched our camels in a hollow, hurriedly tying their knees to stop them from rising, and then climbed a dune to get above the raiders. We crawled to the dune-crest, and I peeped round a clump of tribulus. Three camels were

We had a saluki with us, which I had borrowed from Zayid; but he was still too young to catch a full-grown hare, although he managed to catch an occasional leveret. My companions said disgustedly that he was not worth his keep. They had expected great things of him. But they played with him, and allowed him to lie on their blankets and drink from our dishes, for, although dogs are unclean to Muslims, the Bedu do not count a saluki as a dog. A middle-aged Rashid called Salih and his son were travelling with us as far as Dhafara, and this boy was more successful than the saluki in catching hares.

couched in a hollow two hundred yards away. I could see two men lying behind a small dune. A third man, still mounted, was driving off the captured camels and was about four hundred yards away. I could not see the fourth man and wondered if he could see me. Bin al Kamam was a few yards to my right. He signed to bin Tahi, who rode forward shouting. I could make out odd words. 'Rashid . . . Awamir . . . friends . . . otherwise enemies.' The raiders shouted back, and bin al Kamam said 'They are friends. They are from the Manahil.' The man whom I had been unable to see got up from behind a bush, went forward and spoke to bin Tahi, who then rode back to us. He said, 'It is Jumaan.' I knew that Jumaan bin Duailan was the brother of 'The Cat' whom the Yam had killed the year before, and that he was the worst outlaw in these parts. I had seen him in the spring at Zayid's fort, a small man like his brother, with the same quick, restless eyes. We went over to them, greeted them, and exchanged the news. They had taken the camels from the Manasir. The Manahil were allies of the Rashid, and the Manasir were no concern of ours, but bin al Kamam whispered to me, 'Offer them twenty-five *riyals* to return the camels. Zayid will be pleased if you recover them.' Jumaan, however, refused the offer, knowing that we would not take them by force. They said good-bye, mounted their camels, and rode off. Later, when I was back at Muwaiqih telling Zayid about this pursuit, he said, 'By God, Umbarak, you could have had the pick of my camels if you had killed Jumaan. He is the most troublesome of all these brigands.'

The others arrived an hour later, having missed the raiders when they changed their direction. We chaffed them for deserting us. They were disappointed that the raiders had not been Bani Kitab, for there was blood between them and the Rashid. They had counted on getting their camels and also the looted stock which would by tribal custom have belonged to them. Bin Kabina said regretfully, 'I thought I should get two camels'; but I teased him, 'You would have got nothing. We should have killed them and divided the camels between us long before you turned up.'

We camped where we were, and Amair, bin Ghabaisha, and Salih went back with the camels to get our things, returning next morning.

We were now on the edge of Liwa. I was glad that we were travelling slowly, for I had broken a rib wrestling with bin Tahi, and the stabbing pain in my side hurt most while I was riding. Salih and his son parted from us when we reached the edge of Dhafara, and bin Kabina went with them. He promised to rejoin me in Muwaiqih, but now he wished to collect some camels that he had left in Dhafara. The rest of us rode northward until we were nearly at the coast, and then turned back to Muwaiqih. We arrived there on 14 December.

We were hungry before we arrived at Zayid's fort and were looking forward to eating meat that evening. We had not bothered to take a spare camel on this short journey, and, being anxious not to tire our riding camels, had taken little food with us. For the last two days we had been living on milk. There was plenty of this as the sands here were full of camels. Just before dinner four Bani Yas visitors were brought into our room to share the meal with us. As we sat down to feed, each leant forward and took a leg of meat off the dish before us and put it on the mat in front of him before starting to eat the rice. The rest of us were left to share the head and some other scraps. I was struck once more by how uncouth and selfish were these Bani Yas and Manasir who lived on the fringe of the desert, compared with the Bedu from the interior.

One day when we had stopped at a shallow well, bin Kabina said to me, 'It was here that we had a fight with some Bani Kitab while you were away. We had raided them and taken twelve camels. It was the middle of summer and very hot. We were watering the camels, which were very thirsty for we had driven them hard, when we saw our pursuers. There were eight of them. We were six, for there were two Awamir with us. Do you see that high dune over there? Look! We left the camels here at the well and started to run up it from this side, knowing that the Bani Kitab were climbing it from the other side. By God! I thought my heart would burst. I got to the top of the dune and as I got there one of the Bani Kitab came in sight a few yards below. I fired at him; he fell down and rolled out of sight. The rest of them ran back to their camels, taking the wounded man with them. We fired many shots at them but were too blown to shoot straight. We knew they would not follow us any further now that they had a wounded man to look after.'

The Liwa, where we rode through palm groves and small settlements similar to those I had seen in the spring at Dhaufir and Qutuf.

After dinner the room filled up with Zayid's retainers, several of whom had falcons on their wrists. I have been told that in England it takes fifty days to train a wild falcon, but here the Arabs had them ready in a fortnight to three weeks. This is because they were never separated from them.

The room was packed with people, some disputing over the ownership of a camel, others recounting a raid or reciting poetry. The air was thick with smoke from the coffee hearth and from guttering lamps, and heavy with the pungent reek of locally grown tobacco. Yet a tiercel, blinking in the lamp-light, sat undisturbed on the leather cuff which protected my neighbour's left hand. I asked him how long he had had it, and he said, 'A week. He is a fine bird. You will see, Zayid will prefer him to the other ones,' and he stroked the bird's head. All the birds in the room were peregrines, which the Arabs call *shahin*. I asked my neighbour if they used the *hurr*, or saker falcon, such as I had seen in the courtyard of the Amir's house at Laila. He said, 'Yes, if we can get them, but they are difficult to come by, and expensive. They are worth twice as much as a *shahin*, which you can get for a hundred rupees.' I knew that this was about eight pounds. He went on, 'In the Najd they prefer the *hurr*, since they have better eyesight than the *shahin*, and, as you know, the Najd is all open gravel plains. I myself would rather have a *shahin*. They are swifter, bolder, and more persevering.' He held up his falcon for me to admire and called its name, 'Dhib! Dhib!' which means 'wolf'.

I asked him how he had got the falcon, and he said, 'Zayid sent me with a message to Shakhbut and on my way to Abu Dhabi I saw a *shahin* on the salt-flats. Next day I went back there with a friend. We took a tame pigeon with us. I had tied a length of string to its leg and fastened the other end to a stone. Then we sat and waited and at last when we saw the *shahin* I threw the pigeon into the air and hurried away. As soon as it had taken the pigeon we returned and drove it from its kill. We quickly dug a shallow pit down-wind of the dead pigeon and about as far away as that wall opposite us. I got into this hole and my friend covered me over with some salt-bushes and then walked off. When the *shahin* came back to the pigeon I slowly pulled it towards me with the string. Do you understand? Good. When it was within reach I caught it by the leg.' I asked him why it did not see his hand, and he said, 'It is easy. A *shahin* always faces up-wind, and anyway it was busy tearing at the pigeon.'

A little later Zayid came in, everyone rose, and after we had settled down again and Zayid had been served with coffee, one of the Bani Yas said, 'Zayid, I saw two *hubara* near bu Samr this morning,' and someone else said, 'I saw three last week.' *Hubara* are MacQueen's bustard, a bird the size of a hen turkey; they arrive in Arabia from Persia, Iraq, and Syria at the beginning of the winter and most of them leave in the spring, although a few breed there. Zayid had told me that his men had found three nests the year before. Now he asked about falcons, and someone said, 'Hiza is sending up two more which they caught last week. They should arrive tomorrow.' Falcons are caught at this time of the year on the coast while they are on passage, and Zayid needed a few more before he went hawking. He said, 'Good — we will get away in four days' time if God wills,' and then, turning to me, 'You must come with me.' I willingly agreed, having always wanted to go hawking.

In the morning Zayid was busy checking saddle-bags, ropes, and water-skins, giving orders about the food to be bought in the local market, and the camels to be fetched from the pasturages, and inspecting his falcons. He said that one of them looked off-colour and was to be given a purge of sugar, while another was thin and was to be fed on an egg mixed with milk. He watched a falcon being trained to the lure. It had only been taken ten days ago, but everyone agreed that it would be ready to go with us. Later, three Arabs arrived with the two birds which Hiza had sent. One of them still had its eyes sealed. A piece of cotton had been threaded through its lower lids and tied at the top of its head, drawing them up so that the bird could not see. As it had begun to feed, Zayid told the men who carried it to remove the thread. The other, a tiercel, had a broken flight feather which Zayid now mended with a splint made from two slivers of gazelle horn. He then branded both birds on the bill with his mark.

Four days later, Zayid said, 'We will get away this evening. I expect we shall be away for about a month. We will hunt in the Sands to the south-west of here where there is plenty of grazing and lots of wells. The Bedu say that there are bustard there.'

A man who was training a falcon carried it about everywhere with him. He even fed with it sitting on his left wrist, and slept with it perched on its block beside his head. Always he was stroking it, speaking to it, hooding and unhooding it.

We reached camp as the sun was setting. The dunes were already dark against a flaming sky where cirrus clouds floated like burning vapour. The slaves had collected bushes and piled them into wind-breaks behind which large fires were blazing. We soon gathered round them to warm ourselves, for the evening air was chill. A Bedu family had already joined us, and soon their camels drifted across the darkening sand towards us, followed by ragged long-haired boys. A couple of goats had been slaughtered and cut up, and large cauldrons of rice were simmering on the fires. A little later the herdsboys came into the firelight. One of them was carrying a bowl of milk, capped with foam, which he handed to Zayid before sitting down in our circle to wait for dinner. They told us that they had found the fresh tracks of five bustard round the well, and tracks, two days old, of others in the Sands near by. Zayid turned to me and said, 'God willing we will eat bustard tomorrow.'

We were astir early next morning. Someone fetched the camels and couched them beside the fires, round which we huddled in our cloaks, for it was still bitterly cold. Zayid called out to ask if I would care to ride Ghazala and I eagerly accepted. Bin al Kamam said to me as he tightened the girth and adjusted the saddle-bags and sheepskin, 'You have never ridden a camel like this,' but I told him that I had ridden her on my way to Sharja in the spring. Then as the sun rose we picked up our rifles and camel-sticks and prepared to mount. The falconers lifted the eight peregrines from the blocks on which they had been perched, looking wet and bedraggled from the drenching dew, and called to the three salukis. We stood behind our mounts. Zayid looked round to see that I was ready, and then placed his knee in the saddle. Instantly his camel rose, lifting him into the saddle, and we were off across the sands. We expected to find the bustard on the flats between the dunes rather than in the dunes themselves. We walked our camels while we scanned the ground for their tracks. I had expected that we would be quiet, but I might have known from experience that no Bedu can ever keep silent. Everyone carried on a noisy conversation and anyone who got left behind and trotted to catch up broke automatically into song. Suddenly an Arab on the left of the line signalled to us that he had found fresh tracks, and as we turned our camels towards him a bustard rose about four hundred yards away, the white bands on its wings showing up clearly against the red sand. A falconer unhooded his bird and raised it in the air; then it was off flying a few feet above the ground; the bustard was climbing now but the peregrine was fast overhauling it; now they were faint specks not easily picked up again once they had been lost sight of; then someone shouted, 'It's down!' and we were racing across the sands.

As we slithered down the dune-faces and climbed out of the hollows and then galloped across the flats, I realized what an exceptional camel I was riding. I was fully occupied staying in the saddle, but the falconers who rode beside me carried their falcons on their wrists, held by the jesses.

We sipped coffee, while the rhythmic ringing of the brass coffee-mortar invited everyone to draw near.

Later that afternoon we rode away from the fort, past the palm-trees. Zayid had sent the baggage camels on ahead with orders to camp on the edge of the Sands, and now we trotted across the gravel plain, accompanied by twenty-five of Zayid's Bedu retainers, some of whom carried falcons on their wrists.

We came upon the peregrine in a hollow, plucking at the lifeless bustard. One of the men slipped off his camel, slit open the bustard's head and gave its brains to the falcon. He then heaped sand over the corpse to hide it, and lifted the puzzled-looking falcon back on to his wrist.

We killed two more bustard and several hares before Zayid stopped for lunch. While we were baking bread and roasting two of the bustards by burying them in their feathers in the hot ashes, a raven circled round croaking. Zayid said, 'Let's see if a *shahin* will kill it. I had one last year which killed a raven,' but the peregrine which he loosed only made a few ineffective stoops, easily countered by the raven turning on its back.

We rode singing into camp long after dark, tired and bitterly cold, but well content with our opening day. As we sat round the fires and went over the kills again and later as I lay awake under the blazing stars and listened to the restless moaning of the camel herds, I was glad that we were hawking in the traditional way and not from cars as they do nowadays in the Najd.

We returned to Muwaiqih a month later. Bin Kabina had arrived from Dhafara and was waiting for me, but neither bin Ghabaisha nor Amair was anxious to travel any farther. They wished instead to remain at Buraimi and continue raiding camels from the Bani Kitab. I therefore engaged two Awamir instead. Mahalhal, a young man with an indolent manner, had a pleasant, open face, lightly marked by smallpox. Al Jabari was older. He was lean and tall. Sometime or other he had lost a front tooth.

We tried to keep our objective secret, but everybody was busy prying and speculating about where I was going and what was the purpose of my journey. Plenty of people intrigued to thwart me; some because they hated me as a Christian, others because I refused to take them with me, and not a few because they were blood-enemies of my companions. The Sheikh of the Al bu Shams, to the south of Buraimi, warned that I intended to travel in their land, sent Zayid a message forbidding me to enter any of the Ghafari territory; we also heard that the Duru were determined to prevent my passage. Bakhit al Dahaimi, whom I had met in Abu Dhabi in the spring, claimed the right to be of our party, but I had always disliked him and refused. He vowed angrily that none of his tribe should go with me, and when my companions ignored his noisy threats he became vindictive and promised to settle with us in the Sands. We pretended indifference and told everyone that we were returning to the Hadhramaut across the central Sands. Several people said to me, however, 'In that case why have you not bought sand camels? All the camels you have bought are mountain camels. Clearly you are going to Oman.' Zayid secretly sent off one of his retainers, a Mahra called Hamaid, to find Salim bin Habarut, a sheikh of the powerful Junuba tribe, and to persuade him to meet us in the Sands on the edge of the Duru country at Qasaiwara well. He said: 'Salim should be able to take you through the Duru and get you to Izz, for both the Junuba and the Duru are Ghafaris. I will give you a letter to Yasir who lives at Izz. He is the most important of the Junuba; he stayed with me here last year. I did him well then, and I think he will probably help you. You may be able to get into Oman, but God knows how you will get out again.'

We went on again as soon as we had fed, and a little later put up a bustard within fifty yards of us, but the peregrine which Zayid had unhooded refused to fly. Zayid looked up and, pointing to four eagles high above us, said, 'It is afraid of them.' Shortly afterwards we put up another bustard and this time the peregrine took off. Almost immediately it dashed back to Zayid and thumped against his chest as an eagle swooped down at it with a loud swishing noise, rather like a shell going through the air. I was surprised that the eagle had gone for the peregrine and ignored the bustard. Stroking the frightened bird, Zayid said, 'That was a near thing—it was lucky it did not get her. Well, we shall have to go on—it is no use hanging about here with those eagles overhead.'

The Quicksands of Umm al Samim

> *I plan to complete my travels in Southern Arabia by exploring Oman. I travel with the Rashid through the Duru country, find the quicksands, and reach the southern coast.*

The six of us left Muwaiqih on 28 January 1949 with two spare camels to carry food and water. For the first two days we travelled in a westerly direction to avoid the Al bu Shams who were camped along the eastern edge of the Sands and to convince anyone who saw us pass that we were heading not for Oman but for the Hadhramaut.

On 6 February we arrived at Qasaiwara and there picked up the tracks of Hamaid and Salim, who were camping near by. Salim was middle-aged, of medium height, and dressed in brown. Although they were of Bedu origin, both he and Hamaid had lived for years in villages on the fringe of the desert and it was immediately apparent that this less-exacting life had softened them.

Von Wrede was the first European to mention quicksands in the southern Arabian desert. He claimed that in 1843 he had found a dangerous quicksand known as Bahr al Safi in the Sands north of the Hadhramaut. Bertram Thomas was sceptical of von Wrede's claim to have discovered the Bahr al Safi and thought that it would eventually be identified with Umm al Samim, of which he had heard from his guides. I myself had travelled through the Sands where von Wrede claimed to have seen his quicksands, and I was convinced that they did not exist there. Many Bedu whom I questioned had heard of the Bahr al Safi. Some identified it with Umm al Samim, others with Sabkhat Mutti, and yet others thought it was somewhere in the Najd; not one suggested that it was to be found in the Sands north of the Hadhramaut. To me it seemed probable that the legend of the Bahr al Safi had grown out of Bedu stories of Umm al Samim. I was determined on this journey to fix the position of these quicksands, which I was certain were here — 750 miles east of the Hadhramaut.

We arrived at the Wadi al Ain after three days and found a little sweet water near the surface. Some Duru were camped near by. We would have preferred to go on after filling our water-skins without attracting the attention of the Duru, but the weather was bitterly cold, blowing a northerly gale, and

When I first entered the sands I was bewildered by the utter unfamiliarity of my surroundings and frightened by the feeling that I had only to be separated from my companions to be completely lost in the maze of dunes. Now, like any Rashid, I regarded the Sands as a place of refuge, somewhere where our enemies could not follow us, and I disliked the idea of leaving the shelter they afforded. Nevertheless, it was essential to leave them now and turn eastwards across the Duru plains to avoid finding ourselves on the wrong side of the Umm al Samim quicksands.

Hamaid, whom I already knew, was small, dark, and dressed in white.

several of our camels were staling blood. We were afraid that we should lose them if we went on before the wind dropped; here at least there were a few bushes to give them a little shelter.

Early next morning we saw a party of about twenty mounted men approaching, two riders on each camel. They dismounted two hundred yards away where a low bank gave some protection from the wind. They were obviously a pursuit party and we realized that we were in for trouble. Bin al Kamam turned to Salim and asked 'Who are they?' and Salim answered 'God destroy them! It is Sulaiman bin Kharas and others of the Duru sheikhs.' He watched them for a while and then said, 'Come, Hamaid, we had better go and find out what they want.'

The Duru rose to greet them and they all sat down in a circle. Soon we heard raised voices. I suggested that we should go over to them, but bin al Kamam said, 'No, stay here. Leave it to Salim and Hamaid; they are Ghafaris.' Meanwhile more Duru arrived, among them Staiyun and his son Ali, both of whom came over to us. Bin Kabina started to make coffee and someone placed a dish of dates for them to eat in the shelter of our baggage, but even there the wind soon filled the dish with sand.

Old Staiyun said, 'The sheikhs are determined to stop any Christian from travelling in our country, but you stayed with me two years ago and are my friend. I and my son will now take you wherever you wish to go, regardless of what the sheikhs may say.' I thanked him and asked if he had realized who I was when I stayed with him. 'No,' he answered, 'we often wondered who you were and where you came from, but it never occurred to us that you were a Christian.' After he had drunk coffee, he said, 'Come. Let us go over to the sheikhs.' We picked up our rifles and followed him. I greeted the Duru, who now numbered about forty, and followed by my companions, walked down their line, shaking hands with each of them in turn. Then, after we had exchanged 'the news', we sat down opposite them, Staiyun and Ali sitting beside me. Salim and bin Kharas went on with their argument. Salim said furiously, 'The Junuba are accepted as *rabia* by the Duru. By what right do you stop us?' Bin Kharas shouted back, 'The customs of the tribes do not apply to Christians.' He was a thickset man with angry blood-shot eyes, dominant and aggressive. Old Staiyun now joined in: 'Why do you make all this trouble, bin Kharas? There is no harm in the man. He is known among the tribes and well spoken of. I know him; you don't. He stayed with me for ten days and did me no harm. On the contrary he helped me. He is my friend.' Hamaid interposed: 'Umbarak is Zayid's friend. He has lived among the tribes for years; he is not like other Christians, he is our friend.' But bin Kharas shouted, 'Then take him back to Zayid. We don't want him here. Take him back at least to Qasaiwara and don't bring him this way again or we will kill him.' Old Staiyun leant forward and said angrily, 'You have no right to talk like this. God Almighty! I myself will take him through our country in defiance of you and all the other sheikhs. You can't stop me.' I looked at the Rashid. Apparently unconcerned, they sat in silence, their eyes moving from speaker to speaker. Bin Tahi poked holes in the ground with his stick; otherwise they hardly moved. They were facing their enemies and very conscious of their dignity. Finally bin al Kamam said, 'You cannot trust the Duru. Too many people who travel with them die of snake-bite.' I remembered how al Auf had used this same expression when I first entered the Duru country two years before. I wondered how we should get back through their country. Unless we could return through the mountains there was no way round it.

Next morning the wind had dropped. We filled all our waterskins, for Staiyun, who offered to come with us, thought that we might meet with further opposition when we tried to water in the Amairi. I asked him to take us along the edge of Umm al Samim so that I could see the quicksands. He said, 'All right, but there is really nothing to see.' We travelled across interminable gravel strewn with limestone fragments and bare of vegetation, until at last we came to the shallow watercourse of the Zuaqti, defined by a sprinkling of herbs shrivelled by years of drought. Beyond, a tawny plain merged into a dusty sky, and nothing, neither stick nor stone, broke its drab monotony. Staiyun turned to me: 'There you are. That is Umm al Samim.'

I remembered my excitement two years before when al Auf had first spoken to me of these quicksands as we sat in the dark discussing our route across the Sands. Now I was looking on them, the first European to do so. The ground, of white gypsum powder, was covered with a sand-sprinkled crust of salt, through which protruded occasional dead twigs of *arad* salt-bush. These scattered bushes marked the firm land; farther out, only a slight darkening of the surface indicated the bog below. I took a few steps forward and Staiyun put his hand on my arm, saying, 'Don't go any nearer — it is dangerous.' I wondered how dangerous it really was, but when I questioned him he assured me that several people, including an Awamir raiding party, had perished in these sands, and he told me once again how he had himself watched a flock of goats disappear beneath the surface.

We watered in the Amairi and the few Duru who were there did not interfere with us. In order to link up my present compass-traverse with that which I had made three years earlier in the Sahma Sands to the east of Mugshin, I was anxious to visit the Gharbaniat Sands to the west of Umm al Samim. Some Duru had told us that these sands were full of oryx; but in any case the Rashid were happy at the idea of visiting them, since they expected to find grazing for their camels there.

Staiyun left from here to return to his encampment, but first he found an Afar to act as our guide until we reached the Wahiba country. This man offered to take us across the southern tip of Umm al Samim. We all disliked the idea of setting foot on it, but he assured us he knew a safe path which would save a long detour, an important consideration as the next well was far away. We started at dawn. For three hours we moved forward a few feet at a time across the greasy surface, trying to hold up the slipping, slithering camels, so that they should not fall down and split themselves. Often our weight broke through the surface crust of salt, and then we waded through black clinging mud which stung the cuts and scratches on our legs. Incessantly the half-bogged camels tried to stop, but we dragged and beat them forward, fearful lest, if they ceased to move, they would sink in too deep to get out again. Uneasily, I remembered stories of vehicles which had sunk out of sight in similar quicksands in the Qatara depression during the war. The others, too, were obviously nervous and bin Kabina voiced our thoughts when he said, 'I hope to God the whole surface doesn't break up; I don't want to drown in this muck.' It seemed a very long time before we reached the safety of a limestone ridge which marked the firm ground on the far side. From there we saw the Sands: wide-sweeping, warm-coloured dunes dotted with grazing for our camels.

A Duru, whose tribe was unwilling to let a Christian travel in their territory.

We arrived nine days later at Farai on the edge of the Wahiba country after watering at Muqaibara, a little-used well on the northern edge of the Huquf, where the bitter water was nastier than any I had ever drunk. We had emptied our water-skins the night before and had some difficulty in finding the well, since our Afar guide was confused by dunes, three or four feet high, which he said had not been there when he passed that way ten years earlier. To me it seemed that these tongues of sand were the only landmarks on the level plain that we had been crossing for the past two days.

At Farai there was a busy crowd of Wahiba, Junuba, and Harasis watering their camels and donkeys, and flocks of sheep and goats. I had an anxious moment when a Wahiba boy recognized bin Kabina's camel as one which had been stolen from him a few months earlier, but bin al Kamam reassured me, explaining that by tribal custom the boy now had no claim to it since bin Kabina had bought it. The lad was, however, anxious to get it back as it was his favourite, and after a little haggling bin Kabina handed it over in part exchange for a far finer animal that he had just been admiring.

The evening that we were at Farai an old man came up to us. He was one of the two delightful old Wahiba who had spent the night with us at Haushi two years before. He invited us to his encampment, but as this was some way up the Wadi Halfain and as we intended to travel down it to the coast, we declined his invitation. He offered to accompany us, but was old and frail, and so we suggested that his cousin Ahmad should come with us instead. Ahmad was the same age as bin al Kamam and rather similar to him in appearance. He had recently been to Riyadh with a large party of Wahiba to sell camels. His party had suffered severely from fever and eleven of them had died on the way home. He told us later that the funeral feasts had lasted for many days and that a very large number of animals had been slaughtered. I liked Ahmad as soon as I saw him. Not only was he welcoming and friendly, as were all the Wahiba we met, but he had great personal charm. My Rashid liked him too, and bin Kabina said, 'Let us try to persuade him to stay with us until we get back to Muwaiqih.'

We watered again at Haij near the southern coast. From there we should have been able to see Masira Island, by which I could have checked my position, but a gale was blowing and the air was thick with flying sand. We had bought a camel and had slaughtered her the previous evening. She had a large, suppurating abscess on one of her feet, but bin al Kamam assured me that this would not affect the rest of the meat. In any case, I was too hungry to be fastidious. We hung the strips of raw meat to dry in some bushes and I watched with increasing irritation how the grains of sand formed an ever-thickening crust over them.

A cheerful young Wahiba.

The Wahiba Sands

From the southern coast I visit the Wahiba Sands, and then, with the Imam's permission, return through Oman to Buraimi.

We had crossed southern Arabia from the Arabian Gulf to the Indian Ocean, travelling along the edge of the Empty Quarter, but this was the sort of journey to which I was by now well accustomed. From here, however, we had to get back through Oman, a journey which, to be successful, would require diplomacy rather than physical endurance.

I explained to Ahmad that I wished to travel northwards to the Wadi Batha and then to return to Muwaiqih along the foot of the mountains. This route would take me across the Wahiba Sands which I was particularly anxious to see, since they were separated from the Sands of the Empty Quarter by more than a hundred and fifty miles of gravel plain. Ahmad said, 'You are free to go wherever you wish in the country of the Wahiba. We are your friends, Umbarak; none of us would try to stop you. But the tribes under the mountains are different; they will certainly make trouble if they find out who you are, just as the Duru did. Anyway, they are all governed by the Imam and they will be afraid to let you pass without his permission. It's different in the desert; there we could perhaps take you through the land of our enemies, travelling as raiders travel and avoiding the wells. But that is impossible in the mountains; the country is too narrow; we should have to use the paths, and they go through the villages; we could never keep out of sight. I will take you as far as I can, but just you and one of your companions. We will leave the others in the Wadi Halfain and come back to them as soon as we have been as far as the Wadi Batha. But how you are going to get to Muwaiqih from here I don't know.

Next day we crossed into the Wadi Andam, and following it northward we arrived two days later at Nafi. Ahmad now found us a man of the Al Hiya, called Sultan, who agreed to guide us across the sands to the Wadi Batha. I decided to take bin Kabina with me, arranging to meet the others a little farther to the north in the Wadi Halfain, where the grazing was said to be better.

I hired a fresh camel from Sultan; bin Kabina rode his own, and both Sultan and Ahmad were well mounted. We were riding four of the finest camels in Arabia and if necessary could travel

Then, as we were going on, he asked, 'Have you seen an old grey camel in calf?' Ahmad said 'No.' He thought a moment, and added, 'We passed the tracks of a young camel a little way back, and of three camels before that, none of them in calf.' Sultan asked, 'What are her tracks like?' The boy replied, 'She turns her near fore-foot in a little.' Bin Kabina exclaimed, 'Yes! don't you remember we crossed her tracks beyond that patch of light-coloured sand in the last valley? She had climbed the slope on our right and fed on some qassis. It was just before we came to the broken abal bush.' The others agreed that these must be the tracks of the boy's camel, and described to him where to find them. The place was about three miles away. Sultan said, 'God willing, you will easily find her. The tracks we saw were fresh, made after the sun had risen.' The boy thanked us and turned back down the valley. Sultan said, 'Ahmad, do you remember old Salih? He died last autumn. That is his son, a good boy.'

both fast and far. At first we crossed a gravel plain, sprinkled with sand of a reddish tint, and broken up by small limestone tables among which we saw many gazelle, all very wild. Gradually, as we went farther, the sand increased until it entirely overlaid the limestone floor. On the second day we reached the well of Tawi Harian, which was about eighty feet deep. Several Wahiba were there with donkeys, but no camels. We left as soon as we had watered, for we wanted no awkward questions. We were now riding northward along valleys half a mile wide enclosed by dunes of a uniform height of about two hundred feet.

Two days later we camped on the top of the dunes, two hundred feet above the Wadi Batha. The valley was about six miles across and was bordered on the far side by a narrow belt of sand. Beyond this were low dark hills, and towering above these the stark range of the Hajar. In spite of the haze I could see the peaks of Jabal Jaalan near the coast at the eastern end of the range.

Ahmad and Sultan had brought me across the Sands to the Wadi Batha as they had promised. I hoped that now they would not insist on going straight back across the desert to rejoin our companions in the Wadi Halfain, but would first take me westward through the villages that lay among the foothills. When I suggested this to them, Ahmad answered, 'We will show you as much of the country as we can, but from now on no-one must discover that you are a Christian.'

In the morning Sultan warned me as we started, 'When we meet Arabs don't say anything.' I asked, 'Who are you going to say I am?' and he answered, 'That will depend on who they are.' Bin Kabina pointed to my watch and said, 'Take that off,' and I dropped it inside my shirt.

Sultan insisted that we should avoid the Harth village which we could see farther up the valley. 'We do not want to meet Salih bin Aisa,' he said. 'He is the Sheikh of the Harth and head of all the Hanawi tribes. He would soon discover who you are, and even if he were friendly the mischief would be done, for news of your presence here would get ahead of us.' To avoid this village he led us round the northern tip of the Sands into a maze of bare, broken hills. After travelling for two days through these hills we reached the Habus villages in a tributary of the Wadi Andam. We had nearly finished our food, so Sultan and bin Kabina went into Mudhaibi, where there was a market, while Ahmad and I waited for them just outside the village. They came back an hour later with dates and coffee. We continued down the valley, passing several other villages. Along the edge of the wadi were scattered palm-trees and small gardens irrigated from rivulets bordered with flowering oleanders.

It was a clear day, the first one for weeks, and I could see the ten-thousand-foot summit of Jabal al Akhadar, and seventy miles to the north-west the familiar outline of Jabal Kaur. Around us were many other peaks and mountains. As we rode along I stopped at intervals to sketch their outlines and to take their bearings. Of all these mountains only Jabal al Akhadar was shown on the map.

Sultan told me that from here we must turn southwards to rejoin the rest of my party. Two days later, as we approached a well in the Wadi Andam, my eye was caught by an outstandingly fine camel, fully saddled. At the well a tall man, in a faded brown shirt with an embroidered woollen head-cloth twisted loosely round his head, was talking to two boys and a girl who were watering a flock of goats. I noticed that his dagger was elaborately decorated with silver. Ahmad whispered to me. 'That is Ali bin Said bin Rashid, Sheikh of the Yahahif.' After we had greeted him, he said, 'So you have arrived safely. You are very welcome. Your companions are near my encampment; all of them well and waiting for you. We will go there tomorrow. Tonight we will camp with some Baluchi near here. You must be tired and hungry, for you have travelled far.' Then, turning to Ahmad, he asked, 'Did you have any trouble?' He had steady, thoughtful eyes, a large, slightly crooked nose, deep creases down his cheeks, a straggling beard turning grey, and a closely clipped moustache above rather full lips. It was a good-natured face with no hint of fanaticism, but with unmistakable authority. A Bedu sheikh has no paid retainers on whom he can rely to carry out his orders. He is merely the first among equals in a society where every man is intensely independent and quick to resent any hint of autocracy. His authority depends in consequence on the force of his own personality and on his skill in handling men. His position in the tribe, in fact, resembles that of the chairman of a committee meeting. I had always heard that Ali possessed considerable influence, and looking at him now I could well believe it.

Ahmad fetched Ali's camel, and the five of us rode over to the Baluch encampment near by, where we were to spend the night. It was four o'clock when we got there, but eleven o'clock before we sat down to a large platter heaped with tough meat and dates.

About twenty men and boys collected round our fire. All of them, even the children, wore shirts — for here, unlike Dhaufar, it is not the custom to dress only in a loin-cloth. Ali had told me that these people were in origin Baluchis from Persia, but that they had lived for so long among the Wahiba that now they counted as a section of that tribe. They spoke only Arabic, and I should not have distinguished them from other members of their adopted tribe.

Bin Kabina as usual kept his rifle always ready to his hand. Ali noticed this and said, 'It is all right, boy, you can leave your rifle over there. Thanks to the Imam, God lengthen his life, we have peace here. It is not like the Sands where you come from, where there is always raiding and killing.'

We rejoined the others late the next evening near Barida well in the Wadi Halfain, having ridden nearly two hundred and fifty miles since we had parted from them ten days earlier. Ali urged us to go on to his encampment a few miles farther down the wadi, but, instead, we persuaded him to spend the night with us. Bin al Kamam bought a goat; it was long after midnight before we fed. We spent the following day at Ali's tent. This was only about twelve feet long, woven of black goat's-hair and pitched like a wind-break under a small tree. Among these Bedu tribes there is no contrast between rich and poor, since everyone lives in a similar manner, dressing in the same way and eating the same sort of food, and the poorest of them considers himself as good as the richest.

We were still on foot when we met a party of Arabs, three men and a boy, all armed, leading a string of loaded camels. One of them, a middle-aged man with a scar across his cheek, asked Sultan, 'Is he a Baluchi?' 'Yes. He has come from Sur and is going to Nazwa.' Four pairs of eyes flickered over me again. It was the first of several such encounters, and each time I felt horribly conspicuous, standing there in silence, towering above the others, while they exchanged their news and the long minutes dragged by. Yet even as I waited for my identity to be discovered, I realized that for me the fascination of this journey lay not in seeing the country but in seeing it under these conditions.

Ali's two wives, with whom, as is the custom here, we had shaken hands on arrival, joined us after we had fed, and sat talking with us while we drank coffee. Before we left the tent they produced a small dish filled with a yellow oil scented with amber and made (I was told) from sesame, saffron, and something called *waris*. We dipped our fingers in it and rubbed it over our faces and beards. I met with this custom only among the Wahiba and the Duru, but bin Kabina told me that he had been anointed with a similar oil before his circumcision. Ali warned us that the Ghafari tribes to the north had heard of my arrival among the Wahiba and were determined to stop my going through their country. He said, 'Don't think you can slip past them unobserved as you have just done. They will be on the watch for you now. I told Ali that Zayid had given me a letter to Yasir requesting him to help me, and asked him whether he thought Yasir would be able to take me back to Muwaiqih. 'Yes,' he said, 'I suppose Yasir could take you through, but I doubt if he will. He won't wish to offend the Imam.'

I sent Hamaid to Yasir with Zayid's letter when we were near Adam, a small village lying in the gap between Madhamar and Salakh, two mountains which rise abruptly from the gravel plain and run westwards in the shape of a crescent for thirty miles from the Halfain to the Amairi. I had no instruments to calculate their height but guessed that Salakh was three thousand feet and Madhamar fifteen hundred. The limestone of which they are formed had been weathered to leave no prominent features, and no vegetation was apparent on the naked rock. Both of them were dome-shaped, and I thought regretfully that their formation was of the sort which geologists associate with oil. But, even so, I did not anticipate that eight years later an oil company would have established a camp, made an airfield, and be drilling at Fahud not more than forty miles away.

The following day we camped to the north of Madhamar at Tawi Yasir, where we had arranged for Hamaid to meet us.

Next day we remained where we were, waiting for Hamaid. I wondered what to do if Yasir refused to help us, and half regretted having sent Hamaid to him, feeling that perhaps had we travelled fast we could have slipped unobserved through the country ahead of us. Now we had hung about here too long, but whatever happened we should be able to get back to the Wahiba.

Bin Kabina was sitting near me mending his shirt. It was worn thin and yesterday it had torn right across the shoulders. I said to him irritably, 'Why don't you wear your new shirt?' He did not answer but went on sewing. I asked him again, and he answered without looking up, 'I have not got another.'

I said, 'I saw the new one with the red stitching in your saddle-bags a few days ago.'

'I gave it away.'

'Who to?'

'Sultan.'

'God, why did you do that when you only have that rag to wear?'

'He asked me for it.'

'Damn the man. I gave him a handsome present. Really, you are a fool.'

'Would you have me refuse when he asked for it?'

'Of course. We could have given him a few more dollars.'

'When I have asked you for money you have refused to give me any.'

This was true. Several times he had borrowed money to give away to people who asked for it; twice recently I had refused to let him have any more, so as to stop this incessant scrounging of money from him which he would later need for himself. I had told him that I would give him his money at Muwaiqih. I would probably need what I had with me before we got there. I said that he could put the blame on me, and tell them that I would not give him the money.

Now I grumbled, 'You will look well if we do meet Yasir, half-naked in that rag.'

He answered angrily, 'Do I have to ask your permission before I can give my own things away?'

Hamaid returned late in the afternoon. Yasir and three other Arabs were with him. Yasir was dressed in a plain white shirt and a large embroidered head-cloth. He wore a dagger and cartridge belt, and carried a .450 Martini. Hamaid told me later that Yasir had been greatly embarrassed by my arrival, since the Imam, who had heard of my presence in these parts, had given orders that I was to be arrested if I came this way. Yasir had, however, felt obliged to meet me since I had brought a letter from Zayid. He said at once that he could not take me to Muwaiqih without the Imam's permission, but that he would himself go to Nazwa in the morning and see the Imam, and that his son would meanwhile take us to a place in the hills half-way between Nazwa and Izz. I realized that if we went there, and if Yasir then failed to secure me a safe conduct from the Imam, we should be unable to escape. I asked the others what they thought, and bin al Kamam said, 'If you want to get back to Muwaiqih you will have to trust Yasir.' I therefore took Yasir aside and said, 'Zayid, who is my great friend, assured me that only you, the most influential sheikh in these parts, could take me safely through Oman. I have come to you now with Zayid's letter to ask you for your help. I put myself in your hands and am ready to do whatever you suggest.' I then gave him two hundred Maria Theresa dollars, as a present. He answered, 'Go with my son. Tomorrow evening I will meet you, and, God willing, I will have the Imam's permission for your journey.'

The Wahiba seemed to me to be a finer people than the Duru, in the same indefinable way that the Rashid had impressed me as being superior to the Bait Kathir. The Rashid lived harder lives than the Bait Kathir, which perhaps accounted for the difference between them, but the Wahiba and the Duru lived similar lives in the same sort of country. I wondered if the contrast between these two tribes was due to some fundamental difference in origin far back in the past.

An old Wahiba in Wadi Halfain.

We camped next day within ten miles of Nazwa. The town itself was out of sight, hidden behind a rocky ridge, one of many in the broken country that lay between our camp and the foot of the Jabal al Akhadar, or 'The Green Mountain', a name which seemed singularly inappropriate, since its slopes and precipices looked as bare as the hills that surrounded us. The atmosphere was unusually clear and I could see its entire length. For fifty miles it stretched across our front, its face scored by great gorges — streaks of purple on a background of pale yellow and misty blue. The Jabal al Akhadar is a single continuous ridge, and I could not decide which of the bumps and pinnacles that broke its outline was the actual summit. Ten thousand feet high, it forms the highest part of a range which extends unbroken for four hundred miles from the Arabian Gulf to the Indian Ocean.

Yasir came back at sunset. He had several Arabs with him. He told us that on his way to Nazwa he had met a party of horsemen sent by the Imam to arrest me. He had persuaded them to return to Nazwa, and there, after much angry argument, he had induced the Imam to authorize my journey back to Muwaiqih. The Imam had sent one of his men with Yasir as his representative. I anticipated that this would be some sour-faced fanatic, and was relieved when Yasir introduced me to a friendly old man with an obvious sense of humour. Yasir had also persuaded one of the Duru sheikhs, called Huaishil, to come with us. Huaishil possessed the charm which Yasir so sadly lacked. I knew that accompanied by the Imam's representative, and by *rabias* from the Junuba, Duru, and Wahiba tribes, I had no further cause to worry.

I was very busy during the eight days that it took me to reach Muwaiqih. In the desert there had been little to plot except our course, but here there was a great deal of detail to fill in. Except for the outline of Jabal al Akhadar and the position of a few of the larger towns, the existing maps were blank. I was thankful that there was no further need to conceal my identity, and that I could work openly taking bearings and making sketches.

As we were passing under an enormous dome of light-coloured rock which formed a buttress to Jabal Kaur we passed three men on camels. One of them, a small indignant man, smothered under a large white turban, was the redoubtable Riqaishi, Governor of Ibri. At the time I was riding with bin Kabina, bin al Kamam, and the two Awamir some way behind the others. The Riqaishi had just met them. He had immediately warned Yasir that the Christian was in the neighbourhood, and added that he was on his way to Nazwa to inform the Imam. He was horrified when he heard that I was in their company, and left them without further word.

That evening, encamped outside Ibri, we heard that bin Ghabaisha and another Rashid had been there a week earlier. They had visited the Riqaishi, who had publicly insulted bin Ghabaisha, possibly because by now he was a well-known brigand, more probably because he was known to be one of my companions. Furiously angry, bin Ghabaisha got up and left the room. After dark he waylaid the Riqaishi's coffee-maker, a person of importance in an Arab household, threatened to kill him at once if he made a sound and took him outside the town. There he tied the man up and loaded him on a camel. He then roused a cultivator and said to him, 'I am bin Ghabaisha. Tell the Riqaishi in the morning that in return for his insults I have taken his servant, and intend to sell him in the Hasa.'

When I met bin Ghabaisha he told me that the Riqaishi had offered him fifty dollars for the return of his servant. I asked him whether he accepted. 'No. I sent back word that I realized that the man was useless as a coffee-maker. Had he not left me without coffee when I called to pay my respects to the Governor? All the same he would fetch more than that in Saudi Arabia.' Eventually the Riqaishi ransomed his servant for a considerable sum.

From Ibri we rode northward along the foot of the mountains towards Jabal Hafit, passing through the territory of the Bani Kitab and Al bu Shams. Both of these tribes would have stopped me if they could, but now, accompanied as I was by the Imam's representative and *rabias* from the Junuba, Duru, and Wahiba, they were obliged to let me pass. We reached Muwaiqih on 6 April. We had ridden eleven hundred miles since we had left Zayid's fort on 28 January.

The son of Huaishil, a Duru sheikh who accompanied me inside Oman.

The Closing Door

Anxious to explore the Jabal al Akhadar I return to Buraimi the following year, but am turned back from the Jabal by the Imam of Oman. I leave Arabia.

I returned from England in November 1949 intending to complete my map of the Duru country, and if possible to visit Jabal al Akhadar. At Muwaiqih I found bin Kabina, his half-brother Muhammad bin Kalut, bin Ghabaisha, bin Tahi, and al Jabari of the Awamir. Bin al Kamam had unfortunately gone back to Dhaufar. The others were ready to go with me, but bin Kabina warned me that the Duru would prevent my re-entering their territory.

Despite enlisting Zayed's help to get Huaishil, the Duru Sheikh who had been with me the year before I was unsuccessful in securing protection to travel across Duru country. My aim had been to explore the Jebel al Akhadar, but I was stopped near the village of Bahlah.

We travelled back through the Sands and then across gravel plains through country similar to that which I had seen before.

I was disappointed that I had been turned back when I had so nearly reached the Jabal al Akhadar, for I would have given much to have explored this mountain. I knew, however, that it would be useless to return and try again the following year. Travelling in the desert, we had always been able, when held up, either to profit from the rivalries of the tribesmen, or, if turned back, to reach our destination from another direction. The Rashid who accompanied me were Bedu, at home anywhere in the desert, even in country which was new to them or where the tribes were hostile, but they knew nothing of either the Jabal al Akhadar or of the Arabs who lived there.

We arrived back at Muwaiqih ten days later, after travelling by night for the last part of the journey, in order to avoid the Al bu Shams who were on the watch for us. I stayed there for a few days with Zayid before I left for Dibai, taking bin Kabina and bin Ghabaisha with me, for I knew I would not come back and I wanted to have them with me until I left Arabia. On our way to Dibai we stopped for a night in an oil camp that had sprung up near the coast while I had been away in Oman. The 'camp boss' told me that they were nearly ready to drill for oil.

Henderson and Codrai were quite willing to treat my two companions as their guests, and gave us a room together. Henderson asked me what to do about food and I suggested that he should make no alterations. As we went in to lunch I said to bin Kabina, 'While I was with you in the desert I fed and lived as you do; now that you are our guests you must behave as we do.' They watched carefully to see how we used the knives and forks and managed with singularly little trouble. They were far more self-possessed than most Englishmen whom I had seen feeding with their hands for the first time. Afterwards I said to them, 'Your hosts wish you to have whatever you want while you are here. They have asked me to find out whether you prefer to eat our food or whether you would rather have Arab meals.' Bin Kabina smiled and answered, 'We shall, it is true, be more comfortable and able to eat more if we feed as we are accustomed, but, Umbarak, do not mention this if it would cause embarrassment. We don't know your customs, and you must help us now as we helped you in the desert.'

At the oil camp where we had stopped for a night on our way to Dibai, bin Kabina and bin Ghabaisha had not been allowed to share the empty tent which had originally been allocated to me in the 'European lines', and I had therefore spent the night with them in the 'native lines'.

On our first day there bin Kabina accidentally shut himself up in the sitting-room and was unable to get out until he attracted my attention by hammering on the wall; but soon both of them were perfectly at home and were fiddling with the wireless and playing Henderson's gramophone. Henderson and Codrai were endlessly good-natured, particularly as in the early morning it amused my companions, who got up at dawn, to burst into their rooms exhorting them. 'Up and pray! Up and pray!' as they beat the beds with their camel-sticks.

One morning they came back before breakfast from the *suq* in a state of great excitement. As they buckled on their cartridge-belts they told me that a kinsman of theirs had been arrested by the Sheikh of Sharja and that they must go immediately to his assistance. I asked how they proposed to get to Sharja, which was twelve miles away, and bin Ghabaisha said, 'We will hire a car; give us some money; you know how much a car will cost.' I suggested that they should wait and get a lift in a lorry which I knew Henderson was sending there later in the morning, but they were impatient: 'We cannot wait; we must go now, at once. Tell Henderson to send the lorry now.' I asked, 'Who is the man? Do I know him? What is his name?' and bin Kabina said, 'I don't know his name, but he is a kinsman of ours. Is that not enough?' 'Is he a Rashid?' I asked. 'No, he is a Sharaifi.' By now I knew enough of tribal geneologies to realise that this small and obscure tribe was only very distantly connected with the Rashid, but bin Ghabaisha said, 'What does it matter? He is a kinsman and in trouble; we must go to his help. Would you have us desert him, Umbarak, when there is no-one else to help him?'

They went off in the lorry and came back in the evening. The man had been released before they got to Sharja.

Having come to Dibai by car they had no camels to worry about and were content to remain for a while enjoying this new experience. It would give them something to talk about when they got back to the desert. I asked bin Kabina if he would care to live here permanently, and he said, 'No. This is no life for a man. What is there to do?' I noticed that when they chatted together in the evenings it was of the desert that they spoke, rather than of the things they had seen during the day.

Previous pages: In Dibai, we stayed with Edward Henderson and his assistant, Ronald Codrai, in their house beside the harbour, which happily was still unchanged.

While in Dibai, bin Kabina and bin Ghabaisha found it pleasant to sit about, fully fed, and with nothing to do but wander into the suq and gossip in the shops.

We dined that night with the Sheikh of Dibai on the far side of the creek. The lad I hired to row us over asked if he should wait to bring us back and I told him to return at ten o'clock. As we were coming back to the landing-stage bin Ghabaisha suddenly said, 'Umbarak, we have done an awful thing,' and when I asked what was wrong he answered, 'We have forgotten to bring back any food for our travelling companion.' Puzzled, I asked whom he meant, and he said, 'The boy who brought us over.' I assured him that the boy would not expect it, as the customs of the town were different from the customs of the desert, but bin Ghabaisha shook his head and said, 'We are Bedu. He was our travelling companion. Did he not bring us here? and we forgot him. We have fallen short.'

Knowing that I should not come back, I advised bin Kabina and bin Ghabaisha to return to their homelands in the south as soon as the weather got cool. Already they had many blood-feuds on their hands, and I feared that they would inevitably be killed if they remained in these parts. The following year I heard that bin Kabina had collected his camels and gone back to Habarut; bin Ghabaisha, however, remained on the Trucial Coast, where his reputation became increasingly notorious.

One evening the Political Officer who had taken over from Noel Jackson came to dinner. He led me aside and said, 'I am afraid, Thesiger, that I have a rather embarrassing duty to perform. The Sultan of Muscat, His Highness Sayid Saiyid Bin Taimur, has demanded that we should cancel your Muscat visa. I have been instructed to do so by the Political Resident. I am afraid I must therefore have your passport.' I replied, 'All right, I'll get it; but you realize I've never had a Muscat visa.'

Henderson wrote and told me how he was woken in the early hours to find bin Ghabaisha on his doorstep seeking sanctuary with a badly-wounded man in his arms. They had been raiding camels on the outskirts of the town. Henderson sent the wounded man to hospital in Bahrain, and bin Ghabaisha went there with him. Two years later I saw a report by the Political Resident which stated that the Sheikh of Sharja had succeeded at last in capturing 'the notorious brigand bin Ghabaisha who had been Thesiger's companion' and that he was determined to make an example of him. I was relieved when I heard soon afterwards that the Sheikh had released him after receiving an ultimatum from the Rashid and Awamir.

Although we joked during dinner about a 'visa for Nazwa,' I realized that it would not be long before visas really were required, even for travel in the Empty Quarter. Even now I was probably barred from going back there. To reach the Sands, I had to start from somewhere on the coast, and I could no longer land in Oman or in Dhaufar; even if I returned to the Trucial Coast my presence would probably be regarded as an embarrassment by the Political Resident. I recalled that the previous year the Aden Government, hearing that I was planning another journey, had sent me a telegram advising me for my own sake not to enter Saudi territory. Although I had no political or economic interest in the country few people accepted the fact that I travelled there for my own pleasure, certainly not the American oil companies nor the Saudi Government. I knew that I had made my last journey in the Empty Quarter and that a phase in my life was ended. Here in the desert I had found all that I asked; I knew that I should never find it again. But it was not only this personal sorrow that distressed me. I realised that the Bedu with whom I had lived and travelled, and in whose company I had found contentment, were doomed. Some people maintain that they will be better off when they have exchanged the hardship and poverty of the desert for the security of a materialistic world. This I do not believe. I shall always remember how often I was humbled by those illiterate herdsmen who possessed, in so much greater measure than I, generosity and courage, endurance, patience, and lighthearted gallantry. Among no other people have I ever felt the same sense of personal inadequacy.

On the last evening, as bin Kabina and bin Ghabaisha were tying up the few things they had bought, Codrai said, looking at the two small bundles, 'It is rather pathetic that this is all they have.' I understood what he meant; I had often felt the same. Yet I knew that for them the danger lay, not in the hardship of their lives, but in the boredom and frustration they would feel when they renounced it. The tragedy was that the choice would not be theirs; economic forces beyond their control would eventually drive them into the towns to hang about street-corners as 'unskilled labour'.

The lorry arrived after breakfast. We embraced for the last time. I said, 'Go in peace,' and they answered together, 'Remain in the safe keeping of God, Umbarak.' Then they scrambled up on to a pile of petrol drums beside a Palestinian refugee in oil-stained dungarees. A few minutes later they were out of sight round a corner. I was glad when Codrai took me to the aerodrome at Sharja. As the plane climbed over the town and swung out above the sea I knew how it felt to go into exile.

Closing page: Bin Kabina, Western Sands.

I have often been asked, 'Why do the Bedu live in the desert where they have to put up with the appalling conditions which you describe? Why don't they leave it and find an easier life elsewhere?' and few people have believed me when I have said, 'They live there from choice.' When I was in Damascus I often visited the Rualla while they were camped in summer on the wells outside the city. They urged me to accompany them on their annual migration, which would start southward for the Najd as soon as grazing had come up after the autumn rains. Only in the desert, they declared, could a man find freedom. It must have been this same craving for freedom which induced tribes that entered Egypt at the time of the Arab conquest to pass on through the Nile valley into the interminable desert beyond, leaving behind them the green fields, the palm groves, the shade and running water, and all the luxury which they found in the towns they had conquered.

Index